The Picture File

in School, College, and Public Libraries

Revised and Enlarged Edition

BY

NORMA OLIN IRELAND

Author, *Index to Indexes,*
Index to Monologs and Dialogs, etc.

BOSTON
F. W. FAXON COMPANY, Inc.

1952

PRINTED IN THE UNITED STATES OF AMERICA

To the Fethersons: George, Della and Margaret
"A friend in need is a friend indeed"—English proverb

TABLE OF CONTENTS

The Picture File

in

School, College, and Public Libraries

FOREWORD

This work is a revision of the earlier volume, *The Picture File,* published in 1935. It has been undertaken at the request of the publisher, due to the continuance of orders for the book after the first edition was exhausted.

During the sixteen years since the publication of the first work, the writer has worked with picture files in three other libraries and has observed files in many others. This added experience has confirmed belief in our original purpose: a simple guide suitable for the average library, using headings that have proved their usefulness. The headings are neither entirely general nor entirely specific but a combination of both — which arrangement has seemed to work out for the best. In most cases, however, geographical headings are specific because they have proved most useful.

We have added some 375 more headings, including up-to-date geographical names and current subjects which are necessary. We have expanded several subdivisions, some in answer to particular requests from users of our guide, and have made a few changes in the original list where expansion or change seemed advisable.

We have requested picture catalogs from over 100 different picture publishers; we offer you a selected list especially recommended for your consideration. We have compiled a list of picture indexes and bibliographies which we have also included for your use. We have examined hundreds of magazines and have noted those which are especially worthwhile for clipping purposes. These and many more additional helps have been added to the new edition.

Again we say that the resourcefulness of the individual librarian is all-essential, and the successful use of this book is dependent on its application to local problems and needs.

We wish to thank Miss Maria Kirkgaard, head of the Art Department of the Pasadena Public Library, and Mrs. Alpha Russell, Head of the Picture Department of the Los Angeles Public Library for their courtesy in showing their picture collections and explaining their methods.

N. O. I.

CHAPTER I

How to Begin

The first problem of the librarian who wishes to start a picture file is just how to begin. She may have boxes of pictures already cut, she may have stacks of magazines ready to cut, or she may have no pictures at all. In any case, how to begin the actual file is her problem.

1. SOURCES

How does a library get its pictures? First of all, it should "look to itself." Discarded books and magazines are the chief sources to which every library has access. Advertising material, rotogravure sections of newspapers, and catalogs also contain many worthwhile pictures. Travel circulars, announcements of book publishers, pamphlets and pictures from publishing companies are other sources. The last mentioned, however, although of slight cost, need not be resorted to until all the free material is obtained.

Discarded Books and Magazines

Books, of course, contain pictures of all kinds. To mention a few types of pictures found in books — there are illustrations by famous painters, nature study pictures, geographical views, art studies, portraits, etc. Care should be exercised, however, in tearing or cutting out the pictures, as sometimes the inner margin is very narrow and a slight jerk is likely to tear the picture. A razor blade or other sharp knife should be used.

Magazines are perhaps the chief source of picture material. Historical as well as current material may be found in any number of magazines. Any discarded periodical that contains pictures is worth examination. Some of the best to clip (if you have duplicates) are the following:

The Alaska Sportsman	Antiques
American Artist	Apollo
American Home	Architectural Forum
Américas	Architectural Record

Arizona Highways
Art et Décoration
Art News
Arts and Decoration
Asia
Australia
Collier's Weekly
The Connoisseur
The Desert Magazine
Design
Fortune
Harper's Weekly (1851–1916)
The Highway Traveler
House and Garden
House Beautiful
Hoy
Illustrated London News
L'Illustration
Japan
Japan in Pictures
Japan Today and Tomorrow
Life
Look
Magazine of Art
Manana

Mentor (no longer published)
Musical America
National Geographic Magazine
Natural History
Nature Magazine
New York Times Sunday Magazine section
Pacific Pathways
Punch
Saturday Evening Post
School Arts Magazine
The Studio
Survey Graphic
Theatre Arts Monthly
Travel
Women's magazines
  Good Housekeeping
  Harper's Bazaar
  Ladies Home Journal
  McCalls
  Vogue
  Woman's Home Companion
etc.

Advertising Material

A librarian receives all kinds of advertising matter, much of it worthless. By examining this material carefully, however, many pictures can be found that are usable.

Newspapers and Catalogs

The paper on which newspapers is printed is usually of poor quality, and not worth saving. The rotogravure sections, however, are of better quality and may well be clipped.

Catalogs are of various kinds. Seed catalogs, for instance, are especially useful for colored pictures of flowers, fruits, vegetables, etc. College catalogs may be clipped for views of college campuses. For book catalogs, see heading "Announcements of book publishers."

Travel Circulars

Travel circulars furnish an excellent start for a collection since they consist of a wealth of current pictures on all countries of the world. Geographical views are essential in any picture collection (school libraries, especially), and therefore there should be a representative number in the file as soon as possible.

In sending for these travel circulars, a word of warning should be given. Do not write to more than one or two general companies at one time, unless you want to be deluged with mail. Below is a list of companies that will send you plenty of circulars. We suggest you check *Holiday* for further names, including those of the various states which are not included in our list.

Air France, 683 Fifth Ave., N. Y. 22, N. Y.
American Airlines, Inc. (major cities)
American Export Lines, 39 Broadway, N. Y. 6, N. Y.
American Express Travel Service, 65 Broadway, N. Y. 6, N. Y.
Baltimore & Ohio Railroad, Baltimore, Md.
The Bermuda Trade Development Board, 620 Fifth Ave., N. Y. 20, N. Y.
Braniff International Airways (N. Y., Los Angeles)
British Overseas Airways Corp., 420 Madison Ave., N. Y. 17, N. Y.
British Railways, 9 Rockefeller Plaza, N. Y. 20, N. Y.
British Travel Assoc. (Centre), 336 Madison Ave., N. Y. 17, N. Y.
Burlington Travel Bureau, 547 W. Jackson Blvd., Chicago 6, Ill.
Canada Steamship Lines (major cities)
Canadian Govt. Travel Bureau, Ottawa, Canada
Canadian National (major cities)
Canadian Pacific (major cities)

Chicago & Southern Air Lines, Inc., Municipal Airport, Memphis, Tenn.

Cuban Tourist Comm., 122 E. 42nd St., N. Y., N. Y.

Detroit and Cleveland Navigation Co., 1208 Griswold Bldg., Detroit 26, Mich.

French Line (major cities)

French National Tourist Office (major cities)

German Tourist Information Office, 11 W. 42nd St., N. Y. 18, N. Y.

Grace Line, 10 Hanover Square, N. Y., N. Y.

Gray Line Sight-Seeing Companies Assoc., 10 N. LaSalle St., Chicago 2, Ill.

Great Northern Railway, St. Paul, Minn.

Greyhound Information Center, 105 W. Madison St., Chicago 2, Ill.

Haitian Inf. Bureau, 10 E. 52nd St., N. Y. 22, N. Y.

Holland-America Line, 29 Broadway, N. Y. 6, N. Y.

Jamaica Tourist Trade Development Bd., 400 Madison Ave., N. Y. 17, N. Y

Katy Lines, Railway Exchange Bldg., St. Louis 1, Mo.

Linjebuss, Dept. A., 630 Fifth Ave., N. Y. 20, N. Y.

Matson Line Offices (major cities)

The Milwaukee Road, 935 Union Station, Chicago 6, Ill.

Missouri Pacific Lines, 1601 Mo. Pacific Bldg., St. Louis 3, Mo.

Moore-McCormack Lines, 5 Broadway, N. Y. 4, N. Y.

National Trailways Bus System, 185 N. Wabash Ave., Chicago, Ill.

New York Central, 466 Lexington Ave., N. Y. 17, N. Y.

Northern Great Lakes Area Council, P. O. Box, 5439, Chicago, Ill.

Northern Pacific, 338 Northern Pacific R. R., St. Paul 1, Minn.

Olsen Travel Organization, 39 S. LaSalle St., Chicago 3, Ill.

Pan American (major cities)

Philippine Air Lines (major cities)

Rock Island Lines, 723 LaSalle St. Station, Chicago 5, Ill.

Sabrena Belgian Airlines, 422 Madison Ave., N. Y. 17, N. Y.

Santa Fé System Lines, 80 E. Jackson Blvd., Chicago 4, Ill.

Scandinavian Airlines System (major cities)

Southern Pacific, 310 S. Michigan Ave., Chicago 4, Ill.

Standard Fruit & Steamship Co., 11 Broadway, N. Y., N. Y.

Swissaire, KLM Royal Dutch Airlines, 572 Fifth Ave., N. Y. 19, N. Y.

T.W.A. Trans World Airline (major cities)

Tanner Gray Line, 1207 W. 3d St., Los Angeles, Calif.

Trinidad & Tobago Tourist Board, 122 E. 42nd St., N. Y. 17, N. Y.

Union Pacific Railroad, Omaha 2, Nebraska

United Air Lines, Vacation Bureau, Room 207, 5959 S. Cicero Ave., Chicago 28, Ill.

United Aircraft Corp., East Hartford, Conn.

Announcements of Book Publishers; Pamphlets

Publishers' announcements include general catalogs, booklets on authors and sample pages of books, much of which is valuable for picture material.

Pamphlets may often contain valuable pictures, in which case they should be purchased in duplicate. Especially valuable are booklets on various industries and products, such as coffee, tea, rubber, etc.

Publishers of Pictures

Pictures, books of pictures, and postcards may be secured from a great number of publishers, many of whom handle art prints exclusively. We requested picture catalogs and information from over 100 different picture agencies; we offer you a selected list of those received with a brief notation of items, by no means complete, to give you an idea of their specialties especially recommended for your consideration. In writing any of the following firms, ask for catalogs or lists quoting present prices.

Picture Agencies

(Including Commercial Firms, Museums and
Publishers of Encyclopedias)

American Classical League. Service Bureau. Vanderbilt Univ., Nashville, Tenn.
(Rome and Romans; classical mythology)

Art Education, Inc. (Brown-Robertson Co., 6 E. 34th St., N. Y. 16, N. Y.
(Museum color prints; black and white prints; color reproductions of masterpieces; drawings of the masters; historic designs in color; color prints of Jessie Willcox Smith)

Art Institute of Chicago, Michigan Ave. & Adams St., Chicago, Ill.
(Color prints; postcards; various sizes)

Art Lore, Inc., 6 E. 34th St., N. Y. 16, N. Y.
(Religious pictures; modern Audubon series)

Artext Prints, Inc., Westport, Conn.
(Artext prints; color reproductions; catalog)

Associated Publishers, Inc., 1538 Ninth St., N. W., Washington 1, D. C.
(Negroes and negro life)

The Bettmann Archive, 215 E. 57th St., N. Y., N. Y.
(Pictorial history and research — prices on request)

Blackhurst Book Sales, Inc., 1066 U. P. Station, Des Moines, Ia.
(Visual aid units)

Bonham, Martha E., 2615 Ashurst Rd., Cleveland 18, Ohio
(Photographs related to English life, literature, history; American photographs)

Botanical Publishing Co., P. O. Box 724, Cincinnati, Ohio
(Trees, leaf prints)

British Information Services, 30 Rockefeller Plaza, N. Y. 20, N. Y.
(Poster card sets; picture sets)

Chicago Natural History Museum, Roosevelt Road &
Field Drive, Chicago 5, Ill.
(Postcard sets on anthropology, botany, geology, zo-
ology, etc.)
Childs Gallery, 169 Newbury St., Boston 16, Mass.
(Paintings and prints)
Colonial Art Co., Oklahoma City, Oklahoma
(Shakespearean illustrations in color; famous paint-
ings; catalog)
Colortext Publications, 646 N. Michigan Ave., Chicago,
Ill.
(Booklets in color)
Compton, F. E., & Co., 1000 N. Dearborn St., Chi-
cago, Ill.
("Compton's Picture Library and Source materials")
Creste-Andover Co., 62 E. 87th St., N. Y. 28, N. Y.
(Sets of colored prints on flowers, taverns, birds, fruits,
yachting prints, etc.)
Dodson, Joseph H., Co., Kankakee, Ill.
(Birds and nature; industrial pictures; American In-
dians; etc.)
Donohue, M. A. Co., 711 S. Dearborn St., Chicago 5,
Ill.
(Birds; animals; Indians)
Encyclopedia Britannica, 283 Madison Ave., N. Y.
(Reprints on art, etc.)
Freer Gallery of Art, Washington 25, D. C.
(Photographs; postcards)
Geographia Map Co., 145 W. 57th St., N. Y. 19, N. Y.
(Maps)
Greenwald, J., Inc., 681 Lexington Ave., N. Y. 22, N. Y.
(Small color prints)
Halliday Historic Photograph Co., Hampstead, N. H.
(Photographs of New England crafts, portraits, archi-
tecture, etc.)
Hermann, Erich S., Inc., 385 Madison Ave., N. Y. 17,
N. Y.
(Color reproductions of old and modern masters, vari-
ous sizes)

Hispanic Society of America, Broadway & 155th St.,
N. Y., N. Y.
(Illustrations from photographs on costume, ceramics.
paintings, etc., of Spain)

Informative Classroom Picture Publishers, Grand Rap-
ids 7, Mich.
(Picture reference library, including units of teaching pictures on life in Colonial America, Indian
life, etc.)

International Art Publishing Co., Inc., 243 W. Congress
St., Detroit 26, Mich.
(Selected religious subjects; fine reproductions of old
and modern masters)

Latin American Village, 422 E. Ranchito St., El Monte,
Calif.
(Visual materials on Pan America, California, historic
U.S.A., especially designed for schools, colleges and
libraries)

Library of Congress, Division of Fine Arts, Washington,
D. C.
(Facsimile prints, photographs, etc.; "The selective
checklist")

McKinley Publishing Co., 809–811 N. 19th St., Philadelphia, Pa.
(Maps)

Metropolitan Museum of Art, 5th Ave. & 82d St., N. Y.
28, N. Y.
(Reproductions in color; photographs and sheets)

Morgan & Morgan, High Point Road, Scarsdale,
N. Y.
(Morgan photographs on architecture, American crafts,
modern painting, etc.)

Museum of Fine Arts, 479 Huntington Ave., Boston,
Mass.
("Reconstructing the past"; photographs, postcards,
etc.)

Museum of the City of N. Y., 1220 Fifth Ave., N. Y.,
N. Y.
(Postcard views of early life in N. Y.)

National Association of Audubon Societies, 1006 Fifth
Ave., N. Y. 28, N. Y.
(Bird cards and leaflets)
National Gallery of Art, Washington, D. C.
(Monotone postcards)
National Geographic Society, School Service Dept.,
Washington 6, D. C.
(Separate color sheets on wide variety of subjects)
N. Y. Graphic Society, 10 W. 33d St., N. Y. 1, N. Y.
(Small color prints; catalog)
New York Historical Society, 170 Central Park West,
N. Y., N. Y.
(Postcards)
Nystrom, A. J. & Co., 3333 Elston Ave., Chicago 18, Ill.
(Maps, charts primarily)
Perry Pictures Co., Malden, Mass.
(Miniatures on a great many subjects)
Quarrie Corporation, 35 E. Wacker Drive, Chicago, Ill.
(World Book Encyclopedia unit teaching materials
and reprints)
School Arts, The Davis Press, Printers' Building,
Worcester 8, Mass.
(Design, etc.; portfolios)
Scripta Mathematica, 186th St. & Amsterdam Ave., N. Y.
33, N. Y.
(Portraits of mathematicians and mathematical post-
cards, plates, etc.)
Superintendent of documents. U. S. Government printing
office, Wash. D. C.
(Free price lists)
Taft Museum, 316 Pike St., Cincinnati 2, Ohio
(Postcards)
The Twin Editions, 366 Madison Ave., N. Y. 17, N. Y.
(Fine prints of masterpieces)
University Prints, 11 Boyd St., Newton, Mass.
(Black and white prints; color prints; catalog)
Whitman Publishing Co., 1220 Mound Ave., Racine, Wis-
consin
(Small books on birds, dogs, fish, flowers)

Bibliographies of Sources [1]

Numerous good bibliographies have been published which include sources of picture material including maps, charts and visual aids; among them are:

Bacon, Mary R. Pictorial maps useful in the study of U. S. history. *Wilson Bulletin* 7:121–23, October 1932.

Brown, Betty J. Picture Maps. *Wilson Bulletin* 11: 385–89, 415. February 1937.

Dent, Ellsworth C. and Martha R. McCabe. Visual aids in education; references on pictures, maps, charts as classroom aids. (Bibliography #34.) Washington, D. C., Office of Education.

Free and inexpensive educational materials including sources of visual aids. (Special report #17.) The Quarrie Reference Library, 35 E. Wacker Drive, Chicago, 1940.

Helps for teachers: pictures, posters, bulletins, and other materials available from non-commercial organizations — a revised compilation by Mary Dabney Davis. *School Life* 20:89–9. December 1934.

N.E.A. National Elementary School Principals. 13th yearbook, June, 1934. (Sources of Picture Materials, pp. 470–73.)

Richmond, Edna. Materials of instruction which may be obtained free or at small cost. The Author, Fairmont, West Virginia, 1930.

Sources of reproductions of works of art. A.L.A. Bulletin 30: part II. April 1936.

Standard catalog for high school libraries. (Fine arts section) N. Y., Wilson, 1937. Third supplement, 1940.

Townsend, M. E. and A. G. Stewart. Audio-visual aids for teachers. (Social Science Service, series 2.) N. Y., Wilson, 1937.

---

[1] Ireland, Norma Olin. Picture file pointers. *Wilson library bulletin* 16:258, November 1941.

U. S. Office of Education. Federal Security Administration. State library agencies as sources of pictorial material for social studies. (Leaflet #34.) Washington, D. C.

Visual Materials: aids for publicity and display. (Leads #7, rev.) A. L. A., 1939. mimeo. 50 p.

2. CUTTING

The second step, after your material is collected, is the cutting. This duty may be assigned to pages or other assistants for spare time work; or, if rapid progress is desired, may be assigned to one definite assistant. Although the process of cutting pictures is simple, there are several points that should be remembered.

Straight Borders

Picture borders must be cut absolutely straight, in order to give a neat appearance. If a small white margin (varying from one-sixteenth to one-eighth of an inch, as in a snapshot) is left on each side the picture will stand out more clearly when mounted.

Identification

Identification of the picture is usually printed at the bottom, but in case this does not occur, the surrounding reading matter should be searched. The names should then be penciled very lightly on the back of the picture, or cut out and clipped to the picture. When cutting a group of pictures on one subject, it is convenient to clip them all together at this time as this aids in later sorting.

3. SORTING

For those who have their pictures assembled and cut, the process of sorting, or rough classification, is the next step. But it is not necessary that you have all of your pictures cut before sorting, as you can begin on only a small group. If you are anxious to get your Picture File under way, it is better to start with a small representative group of pictures and get them into the file, rather than wait until all pictures are cut and sorted.

Folders Needed

A supply of letter size manila vertical file folders is useful for this rough classification. As these folders are only for temporary use, old folders may be used (by reversing sides), or home-made ones substituted. Altho other plans may work just as efficiently, folders have proved very convenient.

Headings for Folders

Label these folders with general headings, merely for present needs. In some cases the headings may remain the same as in the final stage, but in most cases they will be changed to more specific headings. Some suggestions for general headings are as follows:

Africa	Furniture
America (except U. S.)	Gardens
Animals	Industries
Architecture	Insects
Art	Islands
Asia	Mythology
Birds	Nature Study
Castles	Needlework
Cathedrals	Paintings
Costume	Portraits
Drawings and Engravings	Sculpture
Europe	United States
Flowers	Miscellaneous

Other general headings may be added, according to the nature of the pictures collected. But do not take too much time making headings for this sorting, because it will delay the more important work to follow. The most essential rule in sorting is: keep your pictures together in general groups and let the specific headings go until later.

CHAPTER II

Mounting

When your pictures are cut and sorted, the next thing to be considered is the mounting. This is especially important because neatness and uniformity in this process determine the general appearance of the Picture File.

1. PAPER

There are papers of many different sizes, colors and weights available on the market. While choice rests upon the taste of the individual librarian, yet there are certain features of art, uniformity, etc., that will largely determine this choice. The recommendations given below have proved satisfactory in many picture collections, and are listed because of this fact.

Specifications

Mounting paper comes in various colors, but the most satisfactory are gray, tan and brown. The tan and brown should be used for colored and sepia pictures, while the gray should be used for the plain, uncolored ones.

Mounting paper usually comes in large sheets, and must be cut to size (See *Size of Mounts*). Suitable paper can usually be purchased locally, but in case the librarian has no local paper companies in her city, we are glad to recommend the following:

The Alling & Cory Co., Cleveland 13, Ohio
> Hammermill Cover, Antique Substance 65: 20 × 26 — 130 M, single thick, $5.85 per 100 sheets in light colors. Recommend sepia and deep gray. Also comes in double thick at higher prices.

Zellerbach Paper Co., Los Angeles, Calif.
> Buckeye Cover, Basis 65 Buckeye Cover: 20 × 26 — $4.75 per C sheets (white; colors slightly higher). Recommend French gray, and tan. Also comes in double thick).

National Card, Mat and Board Co., 4318–36 Carroll Ave.,
  Chicago 25, Ill. or 11422 S. Broadway, Los Angeles
  61, Calif.
  Heavy cardboard for special display mounts, various
  prices.
J. L. Hammett Co., Kendall Square, Cambridge, Mass.
  Write for "School Supplies" catalog. Lists Hammett's
  Art Mounts, Studio Papers, etc.

2. SIZE OF MOUNTS

A convenient size for picture mounts is approximately
11¼ by 9¼ inches. With proper cutting, four mounts
may be cut from each large sheet (20 × 26), with a slight
waste. This waste may be utilized for small signs, etc., in
the library. To facilitate the task of cutting mounts, a
card cutter should be used. Care must be exercised in
using this, however, as sometimes the large sheet is uneven
thus causing the mount to be cut slightly off scale.

3. HOW TO MOUNT

Any good library paste that is firm and not too gluey is
suitable for mounting. Rubber cement is desirable if the
picture is ever to be removed. In pasting the picture, tip
the four corners with paste, rather than spread it over
the entire surface. For the artistic mounting of pictures,
several things must be remembered. Never crowd the
page with too many pictures. One picture is usually sufficient for a mount, altho sometimes two or more small ones
may be grouped so as to form a united whole. The following rules for mounting are according to the principles of
art:[1]

Rules for Mounting

1. The bottom margin should always be the widest, to
assure the proper feeling of balance.
  2. The top margin

---

[1] Trilling, Mabel B. and Williams, Florence. Art in home and
clothing. J. B. Lippincott Co., 1928, pp. 47–48.

a. For square pictures, it is the same width as the side margins.

b. For vertical oblong pictures, it is wider than side margins.

c. For horizontal-shaped pictures, it is narrower than side margins.

3. Mounting several pictures on one page.
   a. Space between the pictures must be less than the margin around the outside, and less than the width of the pictures.

CHAPTER III

Picture Headings

The process of assigning the proper headings to pictures is the most difficult process of all. But if properly studied, this phase of the preparation becomes the most fascinating, as well as one of the most simple.

1. LETTERING

First of all comes the type of lettering to be decided upon. Some form of capitals should be used, as they make the titles more distinct, and thus more easily used in the file. There are many styles of lettering that may be employed, depending upon the librarian's taste. Three-sixteenths of an inch is a convenient height. Lines may be penciled in, and erased later.

The lettering should be made in black ink, but not in drawing ink, as this is difficult to erase.

ABCDEFGHIJKLMNOPQRS TUVWXYZ&$1234567890

2. LOCATION OF HEADING

The best place for the heading has been found to be the upper left-hand corner of the face of the mount, one-eighth inch from the top. Although some librarians might at first think that labelling on the back would be preferable, after consideration they will see the advantages of the front-label system. Its advantages are threefold:

Advantages of the Front-Label

1. *Ease in using file*

When looking up certain pictures, one can leaf rapidly through the subject and pick out those wanted at a glance — instead of drawing out each individual picture to examine it. This is especially true when a particular type of picture is wanted, e.g., colored pictures, etc.

2. *Library patrons prefer this system*

Experience has proved that library patrons prefer this system as it is easy to use. This is true in picture collections as well as in other library duties which the public must perform, such as registration, withdrawal and return of books, etc.

3. *Improves appearance of pictures*

A carefully and uniformly lettered heading on the face of the mount improves its appearance by making the meaning of the picture more clear. In displays, this is especially important.

Of course, if the collection were one of fine prints or valuable etchings, the problem would be a different one. In that case a different grade of mounting paper would be used, and different sizes would also be necessary. In such a collection the pictures might be labelled on the back, or in many cases would not be labelled at all, but given a number instead.

3. GENERAL RULES

Altho the general rules of assigning subject headings are understood, nevertheless there are a few rules that especially apply to picture headings.

Simple headings should always be used. There should not be too many subdivisions in a small file. In fact, there should be scarcely any, except for large subjects such as Architecture, etc. Minute subdivisions such as found on Library of Congress catalog cards are entirely out of place here.

Card Record

Altho a record of headings may be kept by checking the list in this book, a card record is preferable for several reasons. It may seem like unnecessary work but it is desirable, in the first place, because it is more flexible. New headings may be added that are not in this list, especially local (city) names. Secondly, geographical and other cross-references can be included, and these are very essential in using such a collection. These reference cards are valuable to quickly identify places or locate special local material. All such cross-references should take this form:

Los Angeles, *see*
California — Los Angeles

The third reason for card records is so that the number of pictures on each subject can be kept on the back of each main subject card. This is also useful in checking overdue picture charges, as well as a guide for future picture subjects.

"See" and "See alsos"

"See" references indicate that there is nothing under that subject, but that you should see another subject. For instance, in our list, the heading Ceramics is not used, but Pottery is. The cross-reference is:

Ceramics, *see*
Pottery

The main heading card is found under Pottery.

"See also" references indicate the existence of other similar subjects, in most cases, more specific. For example:

Food, *see also*
Berries

There are two main entries here: Food, and Berries. We are more liberal in our use of "see also" entries in the Picture Collection than in cataloging of books, because sometimes pictures (in groups) may be found under more than one heading. Sometimes, therefore, "see also" references may be made from two headings of seemingly equal value, e.g. from general to general, or specific to specific.

Form of Entry

The form of entry should follow the standard rules for spacing, etc., as the A.L.A. rules recommend.[1] This will simplify forms, etc., and keep the record entirely uniform and consistent.

---

2 American Library Assoc. and British Library Assoc. Comm. Catalog rules, author and title entries. Chicago, A.L.A., 1908.

4. SPECIAL PROBLEMS

There are many problems that occur when working with picture collections. Decisions must be made daily that will determine the library's future policy. In addition to proper names and place names, there are other special cases which must be recorded elsewhere. These may be kept in a special notebook, on cards, or on the blank pages at the end of this volume.

Cross-Reference Decisions

In addition to the cross-references in the list of headings, there will be many others which the librarian must decide for herself. Although most of these will be decided without difficulty, some examples of these problems will serve to help the librarian in this phase of work.

Historic Houses, etc.

In the selection of pictures, there are groups containing famous houses, literary landmarks, and relics, whose interest lies chiefly in the person with whom they are concerned. In the list of headings, you will find three headings indicated:

Historic houses
Historic landmarks
Historic relics

The term historic was chosen to include the term literary, thus eliminating the extra heading. The heading is then subdivided by the inverted name of the person with whom the subject is connected, e.g.

Historic relics — Jefferson, Thomas A.

There should be a cross-reference from the portrait of the person concerned. Thus anyone searching for all pictures on or about Thomas Jefferson could easily locate them. The card would be like this:

Portraits — Jefferson, Thomas A.,   *see also*
Historic houses — Jefferson, Thomas A.
Historic landmarks — Jefferson, Thomas A.
Historic relics — Jefferson, Thomas A.

20

THE PICTURE FILE

Portrait cards should also indicate cross-references to Paintings, Sculptures, etc., of the individual. Photographs only should be classed under the main heading of Portraits, while Paintings, Drawings and Engravings, Sculpture, etc., should be kept with their own classification and cross-referenced under Portraits.

In the group of Historic houses, if the name of the person is unknown, then subdivide by the name of the house, thus:

Historic houses — Witch house

If the name of the house is known, as well as the name of the person, make cross-reference from the name of the house as well. Thus:

Historic houses — Monticello, *see*

Historic houses — Jefferson, Thomas A.

Cross-references should also be made from certain subjects in architecture to this group of Historic houses, for instance:

Architecture — American — Colonial, *see also*

Historic houses — (name of person, etc.)

Costume

The subject of Costume is another that requires some decision in cross-references. In the first place, Costume should be subdivided by the adjective of nationality:

Costume — Dutch

Stage costume should be subdivided by author and title of play:

Costume — Stage — Shakespeare — Macbeth

When the above information is unknown, then subdivide by name of character:

Costume — Stage — Mary Stuart

Cross-references should also be made from Portraits to Costume — Stage, e.g.:

Portraits — Modjeska, Helena, *see also*

Costume — Stage — Mary Stuart

Costume — Stage — Shakespeare — Macbeth

Consult pp. 72–76 of this work for Costume headings. We suggest you also study Monroe and Cook's *Costume index,* listed on p. 29.

Sculpture

Sculpture contains many subjects that should be indicated by the means of cross-references. Some of the most important ones are:

Animals	Medals
Bible	Memorials
Bible-Christ	Monuments
Children	Mythology
Coins	Patriotic pictures
Fountains	Portraits
History (with subdiv.)	Saints
Illustrations	Symbolic pictures
Indians of North America	Tablets
Madonnas	Tombs

Classification of Paintings, etc.

The classification of Paintings, Drawings and Engravings, and Illustrations is the most detailed and difficult problem of all. There are so many types of pictures that fall into these groups, that it takes a great deal of study to classify them correctly.

Illustrations

In the first place, all illustrations of books, etc., by famous illustrators should be segregated. The main entry is then subdivided by author, title of book, and artist:

Illustrations — Alcott, Louisa May — Little women — Smith, Jessie Willcox (artist)

The word "artist" in parenthesis serves to immediately identify which is the illustrator, useful for the person unfamiliar with illustrators. If the author and title are unknown, then subdivide only by name of artist:

Illustrations — Parrish, Maxfield

Cross-References

Make a cross-reference from the artist subdivision to the author subdivision, or rather to the main entry, as follows:

Illustrations — Smith, Jessie Willcox (artist)
See also
Illustrations — Alcott, Louisa May — Little women
Illustrations — Burnett, Mrs. Frances (Hodgson) —
Sara Crewe

Cross-references should also be made from the subject of the picture. See list under Paintings, below.

References should be made from the general heading Paintings, subdivided by the name of artist:

Paintings — Smith, Jessie Willcox, *see*
Illustrations — Smith, Jessie Willcox (artist)

So many different cross-references may seem like a useless task and some may question the need. The answer is this: always consider the user of the file and not take for granted that he will understand every subject heading as well as you do. Be as specific as possible and use simple headings, but remember your card record should be a real dictionary to your file.

Drawings and Engravings

The heading Drawings and Engravings was chosen to include Drawings, Etchings, Lithographs, and all other forms of Engravings. The library with a large Etching collection may question this heading and prefer separate headings. It was chosen because it was thought sufficient for a small file and easiest to use. Then, too, many such reproductions are rather difficult to classify because they are unlabelled as to whether they are etchings, etc., and in some cases there is no way of finding out.

The rules for this division are the same as indicated below, under Paintings. All artists should be cross-referenced from Paintings, however, the same as for Illustrations.

Paintings

After sorting out Illustrations, Drawings and Engravings, we then come to Paintings. This is usually a large group, and for the purpose of later cross-referencing and ease in handling, they are sorted into the following subjects:

Animals	Portraits
Children	Religious pictures (Bible, etc.)
Flowers	Seascapes
Landscapes	Symbolic pictures
Murals	Miscellaneous (subdivided later)

The typical main entry for a Painting looks like this:

Paintings — Gérôme, Jean Leon — Springtime

And like this, in the case of Portraits:

Paintings — Fulton, Robert — Barlow, Joel (artist)

Cross-references for the above are as follows:

Paintings — Springtime, *see*

Paintings — Gérôme, Jean Leon — Springtime

and

Portraits — Barlow, Joel, *see*

Paintings — Fulton, Robert — Barlow, Joel (subject)

Titles of paintings should always be cross-referenced. Aids in determining exact titles, as well as identifying painters, are found in CHAPTER V, *Reference Work with Pictures.* Subject references should include the ones listed above, in addition to others which may be added as such subjects appear.

Information File

In addition to the many cross-references, etc., kept on cards, the librarian should build up an information file on certain subjects. For instance, names of artists according to the type of painting, etc., for which they are famous, e.g. Abstract art, Animal studies, Bird studies, Cartoons, Children, Country life, Fantasy, Fresco, Genre, Landscape, Marine, Modern, Portraits, Religion, Still-life, Surrealist art, etc., and names of artists according to nationality, e.g. Mexican, as well as state and local artists. Lists of sculptors may also be compiled, according to nationality.

Other valuable information on many other subjects may be collected. Names of cathedrals, based on the article in the National Geographic Magazine [3] for July 1922 will prove useful. They are subdivided by country and type of

---

[3] Walker, J. Bernard. Cathedrals of the old and new world. *National Geographic Magazine* 42:60–114, July 1922.

architecture. Names of different kinds of pottery, by various nationalities will be useful. In the field of Antiques, a great many useful lists can be collected, such as types of glass, etc.

Famous statues, places of interest, historical events and places will all find their use sometime. The librarian who builds up such lists in her spare time will be amply rewarded by the added usefulness of her picture collection.

Optional Division of Subjects

As a picture file grows, certain subjects grow more than others, and often the question arises, "Shall we divide and make new headings, or continue to subdivide?" Since specific headings are always easier to use, we suggest that you make new headings in some instances. This new edition of *The Picture File* makes a few changes which we have found desirable and others are possible.

In the case of geographical headings, we have included many more specific headings, including the names of each individual state in the United States. Under California, as a typical state, we have also included a detailed subdivision of topics which can be applied to every state, with appropriate changes.

Animals is another heading which may be divided as it grows larger. If you have collected a great many pictures on Dogs, Cats, Horses, etc., put them under separate headings if you wish, but be sure you include cross-references.

Some libraries break up Portraits and have separate files under Artists, Authors, Musicians, etc. This may become very complicated, however, and make your file more difficult to use. We prefer keeping lists on cards, easily done and quickly referred to.

Sports and Games may also be divided; separate headings may be used for Football, Baseball, etc. This is optional with the librarian. We have not done it in our list, altho we have included full cross-references.

CHAPTER IV

Storage and Circulation of Pictures

The logical storage place for pictures is a vertical file. Although boxes may be used temporarily in the absence of a file, the purchase of the latter should be made at the earliest possible moment, because otherwise the pictures may become soiled and torn.

Some libraries prefer different types of storage units; this is of course determined by the type of collection maintained. It must be remembered that the storage of fine prints and large pictures is a different problem entirely. In Campbell and Goodwin's "A primer of library planning,"[1] the minimum requirements of a picture collection intended to serve a city that may eventually reach 100,000 population are given. The authors state that space for a collection of 35,000 mounted pictures and a subsidiary collection of unmounted pictures should be provided.

1. VERTICAL FILE

Although letter size vertical files are satisfactory, legal size files are preferable, because when the picture collection is still small part of the file may be used for pamphlets.

Guides

There are many different kinds of guides available offered by as many different library supply houses. Metal tab guides are recommended for neatness and permanence, but there are also plain celluloided pressboard guides on the market that are cheaper and fairly satisfactory.

2. CIRCULATION OF PICTURES

The circulation of pictures may be a very simple task if the system is completely worked out at the beginning. The most easily administered plan is that similar to the charging of books.

---

[1] Campbell, Donald K. and Clinton F. Goodwin. A primer of library planning. *Wilson Library Bulletin* 20:356, January 1946.

Book Pockets, etc.

A book-pocket and date due slip should be pasted on the under side of the envelope, opposite each other. A book card should be kept in the pocket, just as in an ordinary book. It may be labelled in the following manner:

PICTURES   # 1

DATE	BORROWER'S NAME AND ADDRESS	NO. & SUBJ. OF PICTURES
9/13/33	*John Smith*	*6—*
	14 Adams St.	*animals*

The word "Pictures" in the top left-hand corner identifies the classification while the number in the top right-hand corner (corresponding to the same number on the book pocket) identifies the charge. "Date due," "Borrower's name and address," "Number and subject of pictures" include all the information necessary for records.

Picture Envelopes

Envelopes for circulating pictures are the first requisite. These may be purchased in any local paper-supply house or through regular library supply firms. Or, if economy is necessary, they may be made by hand in the library. They should be made of heavy paper, with three edges reinforced. The flap may have a fastener, or not, just as desired. The envelope should be much larger than the picture mount, in order that it may hold a large group without crowding.

Routine

The decision on number of pictures and length of time to circulate depends on the individual library. If the collection is small, the number circulated at one time may be limited and the length of time restricted to seven days. In larger collections, there may be no limit to the number circulated to one person, and the time may be extended to two weeks with possible renewal. Lenient rules, whenever possible, are to be desired.

CHAPTER V

Reference Work with Pictures

The librarian in charge of the picture file must constantly use reference books to supplement her collection, first for identification of artists and pictures to be placed in the file, and secondly for location of pictures not found in the file. Every book with pictures is a possible source book, and of course the magazine indexes offer valuable current material.

1. INDEXES

We have spent some time in compiling such sources for librarians, in our *Index to Indexes*,[1] which contains over 1000 separate indexes under 280 different subjects. In scanning these subjects, with pictures in mind, the following subjects have indexes which may be valuable to the picture file librarian:

Antiques	Geography
Antiquities	Handicrafts
Archaeology	History
Architecture	Natural history
Art	Ornithology
Artists	Photographs
Costume	Pictures
Entomology	Portraits

Visual Aids

The following indexes and bibliographies have been found especially useful in picture file work:

Art Index, 1929–date. A cumulative author and subject index to a selected list of fine arts periodicals and museum bulletins. N. Y., Wilson, 1930–date

---

1 Ireland, Norma Olin. An index to indexes, A subject bibliography of published indexes. Faxon, 1942.

Booth, Mary Josephine. Index to material on picture study. Boston, Faxon, 1921. 92p.

College Art Association of America. Index of 20th century artists. N. Y., Research Institute of the C.A.A. Index 1, 2, 3, 1933–1937 in v. 3, no. 11–12

Ellis, Jessie Croft. General index to illustrations. Boston, Faxon, 1921. 92p.

Ellis, Jessie Croft. Nature and its applications. Over 200,000 selected references to nature forms and illustrations of nature used in every way. Boston, Faxon, 1949

Ellis, Jessie Croft. Travel through pictures; references to pictures in books and periodicals, of interesting sites all over the world. Boston, Faxon, 1935. 669p.

Gage, Thomas Hovey. An artist's index to Stauffer's "American Engravers." Worcester, Mass., American Antiquarian Society, October 1920

Latimer, Louise P. Illustrators, a finding list. Boston, Faxon, 1929

Life. Chicago. Index, v. 1, 1937–date. Annual

Mallett, Daniel T. Index of artists (international-biographical). N. Y., Bowker, 1935. 493p. Supplement, 1940. 319p.

Mentor index. n.d. (o.p.)

Metropolitan Museum of Art. Index to the Bulletin of the Museum. N. Y., The Museum

Monroe, Isabel and Dorothy E. Cook. Costume index. N. Y., Wilson, 1937. 338p.

Monroe, Isabel and Kate Monroe. Index to reproductions of American paintings; a guide to pictures occurring in more than eight thousand books. N. Y., Wilson, 1948

National Geographic Magazine. Washington, D. C., National Geographic Society. Cumulative index, 1899–1946. (Cumulative supplement issued Feb. 1st of 1942 and every year thereafter)

Shepard, Frederick J. Index to illustrations. Chicago, A.L.A., 1924

Skadsheim topical index to the National Geographic Magazine, with alphabetical and analytical sections. Chicago, Edwin Allen Co., 1939. H. Skadsheim, Berrien Springs, Mich. unpaged

Smith, Ralph C. Biographical index of American artists. Baltimore, Williams and Wilkins, 1930. 102p.

Unpublished Indexes

A large number of libraries have made indexes of pictures found in various books and magazines in their collections. Cooperative indexing among librarians is the key-word of today,[2] and thus before starting any local indexing of pictures, it is well to visit nearby libraries, as well as checking the A.L.A. Junior Members union list of unpublished indexes [3] which includes approximately 8000 indexes from 950 libraries. There are hundreds of indexes on art; here are just a few subjects to be found:

Archaeology

Architecture

Art — Study and teaching

Caricatures and cartoons

Christian art and symbolism

Connoisseur (per.)

Costume

Drawings and engravings

Illustrators

Jesus Christ in art

Maps, Pictorial

Motion pictures — Stills

Paintings

Photographs

Physicians and art

Pictures (many subdivisions)

Portraits

Sculpture

In Appendix II of the same book is a list of books which have been indexed, in whole or in part, by libraries. A survey of this list will save much duplication in libraries.

2. GENERAL REFERENCE BOOKS

Encyclopedias, reference books in history, science, literature and other special fields are all source material for the

---

[2] Ireland, Norma Olin. Cooperative indexing: a postwar program today. *College and Research Libraries* 6:73–75, December 1944.

[3] Junior Members Round Table, American Library Association. Local indexes in American libraries, edited by Norma Olin Ireland. Boston, Faxon, 1947.

picture librarian and should be studied with this purpose in mind. We do not have space to cover this field extensively, but will list a few of the special books which have proven especially useful in our experience. We suggest that a card file be started which will include not only the best pictorial reference books but pictorial books on the general shelves as well. See also list under *Picture Identification for Contests*, p. 32.

American Art Annual, 1898–date. N. Y., American Federation of Arts

Bailey, Henry T. and Ethel Pool. Symbolism for artists — creative and appreciative. Worcester, Mass., The Davis Press, 1925

Brewer, Rev. E. Cobham. Character sketches of romance, fiction and the drama. Ed. by Marion Harland. Hess, 1892

Bryan, Michael. Dictionary of painters and engravers. 5v. N. Y., Macmillan, 1903–1905

Christensen, Erwin O. The index of American design. N. Y., Macmillan, 1950

Clement, Clara Erskine. A handbook of legendary and mythological art. N. Y., Hurd and Houghton, 1871

Fielding, Mantle. Dictionary of American painters, sculptors and engravers. Philadelphia, n.d.

Gayley, Charles M. The classic myths in English literature and in art. Boston, Ginn, 1911

Goldsmith, Elisabeth. Ancient pagan symbols. Putnam, 1929

Harper's dictionary of classical literature and antiquities. N. Y., American Book Co., 1923

Mach, Edmundson von. Outlines of the history of painting from 1200–1900 A.D. Boston, Ginn, 1906

Meyer, Franz Sales. A handbook of ornament. Wilcox and Follett, 1945

Reinach, Salomon. Apollo. Scribner, 1924

Smith, Sir William. A smaller classical dictionary of biography, mythology and geography. Dutton, 1920

Spooner, Shearjashub. Biographical and critical dictionary of painters, engravers, sculptors and architects.
Putnam, 1853
Who's Who in American Art. 3 v. American Federation of Arts, 1935–1940

Picture Catalogs; etc.

The librarian must remember to use picture catalogs in
the identification of artists and their works. Such catalogs
as University Prints, for instance, are invaluable in this
work. In Chapter I, we have listed Picture Agencies,
many of whom will send catalogs free or at small cost.

We have included many reference books in the next section, *Picture Identification for Contests,* under Special Subjects. This as well as the previous lists is selective rather
than comprehensive, however, and the librarian must keep
that fact in mind.

3. PICTURE IDENTIFICATION FOR CONTESTS

The average librarian is practically helpless when it
comes to picture identification for contests. Because she
does not know the books used, she is not only unable to aid
the contester but also is likely to recommend the unnecessary
use of a great many books.

The picture collection is often consulted and sometimes
yields the exact picture needed. But more often the picture
librarian must know other sources, especially of line drawings. Certain of these books may be duplicated and clipped
for the picture file, or in the case of dictionaries, encyclopedias, etc., whole pages may be photostated and placed in
the file.

The writer is an amateur contester and therefore cannot
recommend the books used by the experts. We can, however, list those library books which include especially good
pictures and may be of some help. The librarian should
add to this list and keep a complete file of the best books in
her library on the various subjects, both from the reference
collection and the regular shelves.

I. GENERAL SOURCES

1. *Dictionaries*

Webster's new international dictionary, unabridged. (2d edition is usually authority for words, and many preliminary pictures are taken from this edition. The first edition, however, with pictures in separate section in back, should always be consulted.)

Webster's collegiate dictionary
(Various editions vary: earlier editions have different pictures from later)

Century dictionary and encyclopedia, 10v. ed.
(One of best sources. Other ed. not as complete)

Thorndike junior and senior dictionaries
(Contain excellent pictures, often used)

Funk and Wagnall's standard dictionary
(Some pictures used, especially in editions before 1910)

2. *Encyclopedias*

Contest picture cyclopedia. Contest Publications, Box 6472, Cleveland Ohio, 1950

Chamber's, Nelson's and other old encyclopedias

The comprehensive pictorial encyclopedia. World Pub. Co., 1943

The new modern encyclopedia, a library of world knowledge. William H. Wise & Co. Inc., 1944

II. SPECIAL SUBJECTS

Animals

American Kennel Club. Complete dog book. Garden City Pub., 1938

Animals of the world: Mammals of America, Mammals of other lands. Garden City Pub., 1947

Anthony, H. E. Field book of American mammals. Putnam, 1928

Bridges, William. Wild animals of the world. Garden City Pub., 1948

Carter, T. D., J. E. Hill and G. H. Tate. Mammals of the pacific world. Macmillan, 1946

Davis, Henry P. The modern dog encyclopedia. Stackpole & Heck, Inc., 1949

Hammerton, J. H. Wonders of animal life. London, Waverley Book Co., n.d. 3v.

National Geographic Society. Book of dogs. The Society, 1919

Tate, G. H. H. Mammals of Eastern Asia. Macmillan, 1947

Troughton, Ellis. Furred animals of Australia. Scribner, 1947

Vesey-Fitzgerald, Brian. The book of the dog. Borden Pub. Co., 1948

Wender animal encyclopedia. Oxford Univ. Press, 1949

Art

Adeline's Art dictionary. Appleton, 1908

Harper's Encyclopedia of art. Harper, 1937. 2v.

Mollett, J. W. An illustrated dictionary of words used in art and archaeology. Sampson Low, Marston, Searle & Rivington, 1883

Richter, Gisela M. Shapes and names of Athenian vases. Plantin Press, 1935

Birds

Audubon's Birds of America. Macmillan, 1937

Birds of America. Ed. by T. G. Pearson. Garden City Pub., 1936

Bond, James. Field guide of birds of the West Indies. Macmillan, 1947

Chapman, Frank M. Handbook of birds of Eastern North America. Appleton, 1924

Delacour, Jean and Ernst Mayr. Birds of the Philippines. Macmillan, 1946

Edey, Maitland A. American song birds. Random House, 1940

Hausman, Leon. Illustrated encyclopedia of American birds. Garden City, 1947

Fish

Innes, William T. The modern aquarium. Innes Pub. Co., 1937

Jordan, David S. & Barton Evermann. American food and game fishes. Doubleday, 1902

Lederer, Norbert. Tropical fish and their care. Knopf, 1934

Mellen, Ida M. Fishes in the home. Dodd, Mead, 1929

National Geographic Society. Book of fishes. The Society, 1924

Schrenkeisen, Ray. Field book of fresh-water fishes of North America north of Mexico. Putnam, 1938

Walford, L. A. Marine game fishes of the Pacific Coast. Univ. of Calif. Press, 1937

Flowers

Hausman, Ethel. Beginner's guide to wild flowers. Putnam, 1948

Hausman, Ethel. Encyclopedia of American wild flowers. Garden City Pub., 1947

Henderson, Peter. Practical floriculture. Judd, 1909

House, Homer. Wild flowers. Macmillan, 1935

Mathews, F. S. Field book of American wild flowers. Putnam, 1927

Stefferud, Alfred. How to know the wild flowers. (Mentor Bk) New Amer. Lib. 1950

Wilkinson, Albert E. The flower encyclopedia and gardener's guide. Halcyon House, 1948

History

Hammerton, J. H. Wonders of the past. Wise & Co., 1937. 2v.

Pageant of America: A pictorial history of the U. S. R. H. Gabriel, ed. Yale Univ. Press, 1925–1929. 15v.

Insects (including Butterflies)

Holland, William J. Butterfly book. Doubleday, 1916

Howard, Leland O. Insect book. Doubleday, 1908

Lutz, Frank E. Field book of insects. Putnam, 1921

Musical Instruments

Bessaraboff, Nicholas. Ancient musical instruments. Museum of Fine Arts, Harvard Univ. Press, 1941

Engel, Carl. The music of the most ancient nations. London, Reeves, n.d.

Galpin, Francis W. Old English instruments of music, their history and character. McClurg & Co., 1941

Geiringer, Karl. Musical instruments: their history from the stone age to the present day. Allen & Unwin, 1943

Hipkins, Alfred James. Musical instruments, historic, rare and unique. Edinburgh, A. & C., 1921

Sachs, Curt. The history of musical instruments. Norton & Co., 1940

Mythology

Gulick, Charles Burton. The life of the ancient Greeks. Century, 1902

Knight, Alfred E. Amentet. Longmans, Green, 1915

Rawlinson, George. History of ancient Egypt. 2v. (esp. v. 1). Dodd, Mead, 1882

Tatlock, Jessie. Greek and Roman mythology. Century, 1917

Wilkinson, Sir J. Gardner. The manners and customs of the ancient Egyptians. E. S. Cassino & Co., 1883. 3v. (esp. v. 3)

Nature (General)

Lydekker, Richard. Lydekker's Royal natural history. 6v. Warne Co., 1893–96

Wood, Rev. John G. Natural history. Routledge, 1905

Plants (*See also* Flowers, Trees)

Henderson, Peter. Henderson's handbook of plants and general horticulture. Henderson, 1910

Meyer, Joseph E. The herbalist. Indiana Botanic Gardens, P. O. Box 5, Hammond, Indiana.

Nicholson, George. Illustrated dictionary of gardening. London, Gill, 1887–1889. 4v. in 2.

Stevens, George T. An illustrated guide to the flowering plants of the middle Atlantic and N. E. states. Dodd, Mead, 1910

Portraits

Current Biography. Guide to Who's Who in the News. Wilson Co., annual.

Eichberg, Robert. Radio stars of today. L. C. Page, 1937

Ewen, David. Men of popular music. Ziff-Davis, 1944 (see also other books of musicians by Ewen)

Kunitz, Stanley. British authors of the 19th century. Wilson Co., 1936

Kunitz, Stanley & Howard Haycraft. Twentieth century authors. Wilson, 1942

Radio personalities, a pictorial and biographical annual, ed. by Don Rockwell. Press Bureau Incorporated.

Ships

Bloomster, Edgar L. Sailing and craft down the ages. U. S. Naval Institute, 1940

Davis, Charles G. Shipping and craft in silhouette. Marine Research Soc., 1929

Talbot-Booth, E. C. What ship is that? Didier, 1944

Tools and Machinery

Butter, Frances J. Locks and lockmaking. Pitman, 1926

Hiscox, Gardner. Mechanical movements. Henley & Co., 1903

Kercer, Henry C. Ancient carpenter's tools. Doylestown, Pa., The Bucks Co. Hist. Soc., 1929

Moorehead, Warren K. Prehistoric implements. Robt. Clarke Co., Cincinnati, Ohio, 1900

Trees

Collinwood, G. H. and Warren D. Bruch. Knowing your trees. The American Forestry Assoc., 1947

Peattie, Donald Culross. A natural history of trees of Eastern and Central North America. Houghton Mifflin, 1950

Weld, Clarence M. Our trees, and how to know them. Lippincott, 1928

Miscellaneous

Cohn, David L. Good old days. Simon & Schuster, 1940

The encyclopedia of food. Pub. by Artemas Ward., N. Y., #50 Union Square, 1923

Peloubet's Bible dictionary. Winston, 1925

Rawson, Marion Nicholl. The antiquer's picture book. Dutton, 1940

Smith, Sir William. Dictionary of the Bible. 3v. Murray, 1860–65

Traill, Henry Duff. Social England. Cassell & Co., 1902–1904. 6v.

III. CATALOGS

Catalogs, both new and old, are always necessary to solve picture puzzle contests. Small libraries which do not already possess a shelf of catalogs would do well to begin such a collection. Included should be general catalogs, such as Sears and Montgomery Ward; representative hardware and machinery catalogs of all kinds; dentist tools and supplies; medical tools and all kinds of instruments; drawing supplies; fishing catalogs; chemical supplies; military goods; etc.

Duplicate copies can be clipped for the picture file. Thus when possible, two copies of each catalog should be ordered.

CHAPTER VI

Uses — Publicity

A picture collection is useful in almost every type of library with the exception of some special or technical libraries. School libraries are considered first at this time, but college and public libraries have also proven that picture files have a permanent usefulness in their collections and thus are just as important.

1. SCHOOL LIBRARIES

Since visual education has become so much a part of education today, pictures find a wide sphere of influence in the schools. Teachers everywhere are beginning to realize the usefulness of illustrated matter in the classroom, and it now remains for school libraries to make this matter available.

Visual Education in the Classroom

Addressing teachers in regard to recognizing vital values in education, Herbert L. Spencer said:[1] "Teachers should know that sensory experience is the foundation of intellectual activity and that from fifty to eighty per cent of these experiences come through the eyes. Very few teachers are gifted with the ability of making word pictures realistic. And yet, it is the realistic and concrete that children are interested in, and not the abstract and symbolic. It is necessary that the oral, written, or printed page be translated into a mental image before it means much to the child. Comenius made use of illustrations in the 17th century to visualize subject matter in his Orbis Pictus. Pestalozzi used the school journey or field trip for observation, and Froebel stressed sensory instruction, particularly through sight and touch."

---

[1] Spencer, Herbert L. Training teachers to recognize vital values in education — abstract. N.E.A. Proc. 1930:921.

In the same article, Spencer listed three definite results of the use of visual aids: [2]

1. "That the use of visual aids effects an economy in time in teaching.

2. That the use of visual aids enriches and clarifies instruction.

3. That the use of visual aids develops initial expression."

Use in Teaching Art

Art appreciation is one of the first uses for pictures in the classroom, and this fact should be carefully considered in the selection of pictures. Although this does not mean the inclusion of authentic prints only, it does mean the inclusion of those of reasonable accuracy. Pictures illustrating design, for instance, should be of good design; paintings should be those of recognized artists, and so on. Of course examples of poor design, etc., may be included for purposes of comparison, but they should be labelled thus.

For the art classes, the librarian should collect pictures not only in the field of design and painting, but also pictures in the field of famous architecture, costume, drawings, illustrations, nature study subjects, pewter, pottery, sculpture, silverware, etc.

There is a great opportunity for the school librarian to build up a really worthwhile collection of art pictures, which will be of great value to the teachers. "There are many indications," one librarian states,[3] "that there has been in recent years an increasing interest in the whole subject of art in America. One of these is the space that is given to the subject in current periodicals, as compared with those of earlier date. To encourage this interest offers an opportunity for the school library."

Home Economics

Closely related to the teaching of art is the teaching of home economics. Teachers of these classes often work

[2] Ibid., p. 922.
[3] Brainard, Jessie F. The use of pictures in the school library. *Library Journal* 55:728, September 15, 1930.

in close harmony as their subjects are somewhat related. This especially applies to the college classes in these subjects. The costume prints may well be used interchangeably as well as some of the design. Other subjects to be included for the use of this department include furniture, interior decoration, needlework, rugs, textiles, etc.

Play Production

We also find students and teachers in dramatics working together with the art and home economics classes. In preparing for a play, very often the art department designs the costumes and the home economics department makes them. Here the library's picture collection can be of great help with its pictures on costume as well as illustrations from famous plays. Portraits of great actors, too, are studied for purposes of make-up. Marionette pictures are also useful in the preparation of puppet-shows. In fact, there is scarcely a limit to the usefulness of the picture file to the school theatre.

Aids in Geography

A summary of the rules for picture selection, especially applicable to geographical views, has been given in a recent article of the N.E.A. Journal, as follows:[4]

1. "Their geographical quality.
2. Their contribution to an understanding of the major relationships developed at a specific teaching level.
3. The maintenance of a proper balance so that children will not secure a one-sided view of man's adjustment in a specific region.
4. The inclusion of key items, natural or cultural, characteristic of a given region or activity."

Geographical views usually form the nucleus of a good picture collection. The reason for this is that the demand for them is usually higher than for any other one class of pictures. Teachers of the social studies use pictures of

---

4 Thralls, Zoe A. The selection and use of pictures. *Journal of the N.E.A.* 21:248, November 1932.

various countries to illustrate almost everything they teach. From prehistoric man to modern agriculture — these and many more subjects fall into this classification. Pictures of all the countries in the world should be acquired, if possible, as well as views of lakes, mountains, rivers and other physical features. The costume group here again finds a new use and it should be built up accordingly.

An excellent source of free geographic material is Booth's "Material on geography," [5] published in 1927. Although out-of-date, many of the references are still good. The same holds true for a list compiled in the Chicago Schools Journal.[6]

Nature Study; History and Civics

Pictures of animals, flowers, plants, trees, insects, etc., are all essential to a school library collection. Colored pictures are especially desirable for this type of study.

In response to the question of why she uses pictures in teaching history, Miss Charlotte Eastman of Iowa City says: [7] "It is because I have found that I can add interest, color, depth of impression, and permanency of possession to any event or situation or condition that I wish to impress on my class by the addition of visual presentation to my usual method. For no matter how gifted the user of word pictures may be, there remains a certain element that can be shown better by the brush or pencil and the imagination of the artist."

History pictures, as well as other pictures, must be carefully selected. The type of picture may vary from a very simple cartoon to a famous painting, according to one author, who defines their selection in this manner: [8] 'Among all these the teacher must identify the really instructional

[5] Booth, Mary Josephine. Material on geography. Charleston, Ill., The Author, 1927.

[6] Branom, Frederick K. Free geographical material. *Chicago Schools Journal* 6:216–23, February 1924.

[7] Eastman, Charlotte. Why I use pictures in teaching history. *Historical Outlook* 22:167, April 1931.

[8] Knowlton, Daniel C. The Washington Bicentennial and the history classroom; history reconstructed through still pictures. *Historical Outlook* 23:330, November 1932.

or educational picture. A picture may be so characterized when it embodies a significant fragment of the past, and through its very form and content contributes to the effectiveness of the teaching. The more closely it conforms to what history is, the more likely it is to make a significant contribution to historical study; the more readily it communicates itself or conveys its message to the student, the larger its place alongside the other media, through which we approach the hidden past."

In regard to the two aspects of the picture — its origin and use, he further states that they are not only closely related but they determine each other. "If the desirability of a visual contact with the past be granted," he continues,[9] "if history is something to be seen, felt and experienced in addition to being something read in a book, pulled to pieces, and put together again as an academic exercise, it follows that picture material is entitled to the same serious consideration as in any portion of textual matter. The teacher's initial task is to select the materials out of which the past is to be reconstructed. The picture, whatever its form, cannot be overlooked as he assembles his data."

The teacher of civics is, of course, closely related to history, and sometimes the two are combined in a single course. Pictures of industries, maps, government organization charts, etc., are all valuable for this study.

There are other classes in the curriculum, although not mentioned at this time, which undoubtedly use pictures. Pupils will find them useful also for special reports, speeches, etc. Pictures on every imaginable subject may be wanted sometime, and because of this fact the librarian must truly become a collector.

Displays and Publicity

Although a school librarian may have spent months and months on her picture file, yet without the use of displays and publicity her collection may remain unused. There are many ways of handling this phase of the work, any one or all of which may be suitable.

9 *Ibid.*, p. 329.

Direct to Teacher

"There are two factors necessary," says Jessie Brainard of the Horace Mann School library,[10] "to make such a collection useful: the desire of the teacher, and the active cooperation of the librarian. Some teachers need only to be shown available material, and thereafter come to the library, select what they need and place it on their classroom bulletin boards, or on one of those assigned for teachers' use in the library. Other teachers, who are more pressed for time, or who regard illustrative aids of minor value, never come for material, but are pleased if the librarian keeps in touch with their work and supplies their bulletin boards with appropriate pictures."

Bulletin Boards

A second means of displaying pictures is through the use of bulletin boards either in the library, corridor, or classroom. Seasonal displays of pictures are always appreciated, and do much to make rooms attractive.

There are certain rules regarding the placement of these pictures, however, that should be observed. "Don't frustrate your own purpose by careless hanging," states one authority,[11] "If you put it on the bulletin board, don't insert it in the midst of printed notices, book jackets, calendars, and health charts. While the picture is on the bulletin board, can't the other thing come off? If you hang it from the moldings above the blackboard, see that it is not immediately surrounded by writing or figures. Hang it low enough for the little folk to look straight into the picture. Do not have many other pictures in the room at the same time. When several people talk at once, no one gets his message over. Pictures have something to say. Let them be heard, one at a time."

---

[10] Brainard, Jessie F. The use of pictures in the school library. *Library Journal* 55:729, September 15, 1930.

[11] Israel, Marion Louise. Picture helps for smaller schools — abstract. *N.E.A. Proc.* 1931:955.

Book Displays

Book exhibits are made more attractive when accompanied by posters and pictures. This is especially true for children, to whom illustrated matter is of first importance. School clubs may be requested to aid in arranging special exhibits, which activity arouses their interest. The subject of displays will be discussed further in connection with public libraries.

The School Paper

While bulletin boards and displays will reach a large majority of students and teachers, it is still necessary to get the attention of a remaining few. The school newspaper is the best means to reach that minority. News stories, brief notices and features may all be used to advertise the pictures in the library. Lists of new subjects included in the file, displays and exhibits to be shown are all good material for the paper. In this manner, a steady interest may be developed and fostered, aiding both librarian and student.

2. PUBLIC LIBRARIES

Since public libraries existed before school libraries came to be recognized as such, picture collections probably had their beginning in the former.

Children's Rooms

Although a picture file may be located in the adult section of the public library, the most popular location is the children's room of the library. The collection, preparation and supervision of the file therefore falls to the lot of the children's librarian.

Subjects Needed

Although housed in the children's department, the circulation of pictures extends to adults as well. The subjects chosen, for this reason, should include every field of knowledge. Requests may vary from an artist's request for a sketch of a medieval knight to the local newspaper's call for a picture of the "Union Jack." All pictures have a place in this collection, subject of course to the rules of careful selection. Children's needs occupy an important place, as well as those of teachers who are not served by a school library.

Displays; Window Exhibits

The book display is a recognized factor in public libraries today and pictures may well be used to supplement these displays. Often libraries are given the use of windows in down-town stores for special exhibits and temporary displays.

"The librarian can do little more," says one librarian,[12] "to make the library an attractive place than by the judicious selection of pictures for exhibition. They can be made the guide post which attracts the children to a group of books which otherwise they would not be particularly interested in seeking. They may be the means of interesting a group in seeing things which daily surround them, such as types of cloud formation, neighboring birds, styles of architecture, the shape of trees. A well-lettered and brief note of explanation accompanying the picture on display will aid."

Essential Library Service

Romana Javitz, in an article entitled *Images and words*,[13] speaks of collecting pictorial documents as an essential library service. "When one considers the work of our language," she says, "and contemplates the myriad uses to which these words may be put and then thinks of the millions of pictorial images, likewise potential members of our mode of communication, it is obvious that as the words of our written language, so too a pictorial language is in use. Since libraries concern themselves with people and with their heritage, with bringing to them the record of the past life and studies of man, they should more consciously accept

---

[12] Witmer, Eleanor M. The school picture collection. *Library Journal* 50:296, April 1, 1925.
[13] Javitz, Romana. Images and words. *Wilson Library Bulletin* 18:220, November 1943.

the organization and availability of pictorial documents as an essential library service."

"Your picture collection will make new friends in innumerable ways," states Janet Coe Sanborn in describing her library's historical picture collection,[14] "and add a different service and attraction to your library. It will furnish you with a fresh approach to your patrons as well as a brand-new field for library contacts."

Newspaper Publicity

Local papers are always anxious for news about the public library and pictures may well be publicized in this connection. "A worthwhile picture file is well worth advertising" might be adopted as a suitable slogan for public libraries.

3. COLLEGE AND UNIVERSITY LIBRARIES

Upon first thought, you might ask, "Of what use are pictures in a college library," and feel sure that the answer would be negative. This is untrue, however, because it has been found that pictures play a very important part in such libraries.

Pictures as Departmental Helps

Comparing the uses of pictures in college libraries to those in school libraries, we find them very similar in relation to the various departments. Home Economics, Teachers College, Art, History and Literature are all fields in which the picture file has proven useful.

Individual Uses

There are a great many individual uses that can be made of the collection. Requests of all kinds come to the Reference desk which can often be answered quickly by the picture file. For instance, questions like these: "How do French peasants dress?", "Describe the processes of the airplane industry," and "Find a list of the most important landscape artists," etc.

14 Sanborn, Janet Coe. Your city in pictures, an aid to good public relations. *Wilson Library Bulletin* 22:535,539, Mar. 1948.

Often professors are called upon to give outside travel talks or other illustrated lectures and find that they need pictures on a certain subject. Students need pictures for art notebooks and term reports. Those who do practice teaching are only too glad to get visual aids on teaching their subject. These are just a few examples of the varied needs in the college curriculum that pictures actually fill.

Displays in the Library

Just as librarians in public libraries are trying to direct the wise use of leisure time by means of guided reading, in the same manner college librarians are striving to aid the student. Displays and suggested groups of books are the easiest means to this end, and to attract attention to these displays, what better means than pictures? All kinds of hobby displays can be worked out with books and pictures — directing the student to new thoughts and interests.

The College Newspaper

For publicity purposes, the college newspaper serves the college librarian best of all. A student assistant may be appointed, or one of the staff members may be assigned to write short news stories, features, etc., advertising the library's pictures and displays. But here, as in all newspapers, dull, stereotype articles must be avoided or else the purpose is defeated.

4. SUMMARY

Thus we find that the picture file is an important factor in school, college and public libraries. To quote a librarian who expresses the same thought: [15] "There is no doubt that the preparation and care of pictures can absorb an enormous amount of time well spent, provided the selection is discriminating enough to be a contributing factor to that education which, in the words of Horace Mann, 'alone can conduct us to that enjoyment which is at once best in quality and infinite in quantity.' "

[15] Brainard, Jessie F. The use of pictures in the school library. *Library Journal* 55:729, September 15, 1930.

LIST OF PICTURE HEADINGS *

A

Abacus

Abbeys (subdivided by adjective of nationality, and furthei
by names of abbeys)
See also Cathedrals; Convents; Monasteries

Abyssinia. *See* Ethiopia

Accidents
See also Aircraft accidents

Acrobatics. *See* Sports — Acrobatics

Advertisements (subdivided by class of product)
Foreign
U. S.
U. S. Early

Aeronautics. *See* Airplanes; Airports; Airships; Autogiros; Aviation; Balloons; Helicopters; Jet propulsion; Seaplanes; etc.

Afghanistan

Africa. *See* Africa, British East; Africa, British West;
Africa, Central; Africa, French West; Africa, North;
Africa, South; Congo, Belgian; Egypt; etc.

Africa, British East

Africa, British West

Africa, Central
See also Congo, Belgian

Africa, East. *See* Africa, British East

Africa, French West

Africa, North
See also Algeria; Morocco; Tripoli (Tripolitania)

* See *Chapter III,* 4. Special Problems.

Africa, South

Africa, West. *See* Africa, British West; Africa, French
West; Cape Verde Peninsula; Nigeria

Agricultural machinery

Agriculture
    See also Animals; Dairies; Dairying; Grains and grasses;
    Poultry houses; Stock raising; Wheat; etc.

Air conditioning

Air Corps

Air raids. *See* Civilian defense

Air warfare

Aircraft accidents

Airplanes
    See also Seaplanes
    Diagrams
    Model

Airports
    Floating

Airships

Alabama

Alaska

Albania

Algeria

Alhambra

Almanacs
    See also Calendars

Alphabets. *See* Lettering

Aluminum

America — Discovery and exploration

American colonies. *See* Colonial life and customs

American Samoa

Americanization. *See* Flag Day; Social settlements;
U. S. — History; etc.

Amusements. *See* Dances; Games; Sports; etc.

Anatomy (subdivided by parts of the anatomy)

Andorra

Angels
  See also Symbolic pictures — Angels

*Animals (subdivided by name of animal)
  See also Cats; Dogs; Horses; Zoos; name of individual
  paintings of animals

Animals, Prehistoric (subdivided by name of animal)

Antiques
  See also names of individual items, e.g. Glassware; etc.

Antiquities. *See* Art; Egypt — Antiquities; Greece, Ancient — Antiquities; Rome, Ancient — Antiquities

Aquariums. *See* Fishes — Aquariums

Aqueducts

Arabia

Arbor Day

Archaeology (subdivided by name of country)

Archery. *See* Sports — Archery

Architecture
  See also Fountains; Memorials; Monuments; Tombs; etc.
  Adobe
  African
  American — Colonial, Dutch

American — Colonial, Northern
American — Colonial, Southern
Anglo-Norman
Assyrian
Austrian
Baroque
Beach
Belgian
Bermudan
Brick
Burmese
Byzantine
Canadian
Cape Cod
Caribbean
Chinese
Classical
Concrete
Czechoslovakian
Domestic
Duplex
Dutch
Early Christian
Egyptian
Elizabethan
English
Georgian
German
Glass
Gothic
Greek
  Corinthian
  Doric
  Ionic
Hungarian
Indian, East
Italian
Japanese
Lombard

Medieval
Mediterranean
Mexican
Modernist
Moorish
Moravian
Norman
Oriental
Persian
Philippine
Portuguese
Pueblo
Ranch house
Regency
Renaissance
Rococo
Roman
  Tuscan
Romanesque
Rural
Russian
Saracenic
Scandinavian
Scotch
Spanish
Spanish-American
Stone
Stucco
Tudor

Architecture — Details
Altar
Arcade
Arch
Atrium
Balcony
Capital
Caryatid
Ceiling

Chimney
Choir-stall
Column
Confessional
Cornice
Corridor
Court
Cupboard
Cupola
Dome
Door
  Bronze
  Colonial
  Georgian
Doorway
Façade
Fireplace
Floor
Fountain
Frieze
Gargoyle
Gate and fence
Lattice
Lobby
Marquise
Moulding
Panel
Pediment
Pendentine
Peristyle and peristylum
Pilaster
Porch
Pulpit
Rood screen
Roof
Stairway
Tablinium
Tower and spire
Volute

Wall
Well
Window

Arctic expeditions.   *See* Arctic regions

Arctic regions

Argentina

Arizona

Arkansas

Armenia

Armor (subdivided by adjective of nationality)

Army (subdivided by adjective of nationality)
  See also Costume — Military; Insignia — U. S. — **Army**
  U. S.
    A.E.F.
    Air Service
    Buildings
    Camps
    Engineers
    Entertainment
    Equipment
    Infantry
    Medical Corps
    National Guard
    Signal Corps
    Tanks
    Women

Art
  See also Design
  Abstract
  African
  Alaskan
  American
  American, Early
  Arabian

Armenian
Assyrian
Australian
Austrian
Balinese
Brazilian
Byzantine
Cambodian
Canadian
Celtic
Central American
Chinese
Christian
Commercial
Cuban
Cubist
Czechoslovakian
Dutch
Early Christian
Ecclesiastical
Egyptian
English
Eskimo
Fantastic
Flemish
French
German
Gothic
Greek
Hawaiian
Hungarian
Indian
  Aztecan
  East
  Incan
  Mayan
  North American
  South American
Irish

Italian
Japanese
Jewish
Korean
Malay
Manchurian
Medieval
Mexican
Minoan
Modernist
Persian
Philippine
Polish
Pompeian
Prehistoric
    See also Sculpture — Prehistoric
Primitive
Religious
Roman
Russian
Scandinavian
Siamese
Spanish
Surrealist
Swiss
Tibetan
Turkish

Art galleries.   *See* Museums

Artillery
Anti-aircraft
Field

Arts and crafts
See also names of individual arts and crafts, e.g. Pottery

Asia.   *See* names of individual countries in Asia

Assyria

Astrology

Astronomical observatories

Astronomy
    Auroras
    Comets
    Constants
    Constellations
    Earth
    Eclipses
    Meteors
    Moon
    Phenomena
    Planets
    Stars, Evening
    Stars, Morning
    Sun
    Zodiac

Athletics. *See* Dances; Games; Gymnastics; Sports

Atomic bomb

Atomic energy
See also Uranium

Australia
See also Tasmania

Austria

Autogiros

Autographs

Automatic devices

Automobile trailers. *See* Trailers

Automobiles

Autumn
See also Symbolic pictures — Autumn; name of autumn
painting

Aviation. *See* Air warfare; Aircraft accidents; Airplanes; Airports; Airships; Autogiros; Balloons; Helicopters; Jet propulsion; Seaplanes; etc.

Awards
Literary
Motion picture
Nobel prizes
Pulitzer prizes

Azores

B

Babies

Babylonia. *See* Iraq

Badges. *See* Emblems

Bacteria

Bahamas

Balearic Islands

Balkan states. *See* Albania; Bulgaria; Greece; Rumania; Turkey; Yugoslavia

Ballet. *See* Dances — Ballet

Balloons
History

Baltic states. *See* Estonia; Finland; Latvia; Lithuania

Bands (music)
See also Orchestras

Baptisms

Barbados

Barbary states. *See* Algeria; Morocco; Tripoli; Tunis

Barbecues

Baseball. *See* Games — Baseball

Basketball. *See* Games — Basketball

Basketry

Baths and bathing

Batik. *See* Textiles — Batik

Battledore and shuttlecock. *See* Games — Battledore and shuttlecock

Battles. *See* under names of wars

Battleships. *See* Warships

Bee-keeping

Beetleware

Belgian Congo. *See* Congo, Belgian

Belgium

Bells

Bermuda Islands

Berries

Bhutan

Bible (subdivided by name of character and event)
See also Madonnas; Passion Play; Saints; name of individual painting; etc.

Bible — Christ (subdivided by event in the life of Christ)
See also Passion Play; name of individual painting, sculpture, etc.

Bicycling. *See* Sports — Bicycling

Billiards. *See* Games — Billiards

Biology

Birds (subdivided by names of birds)
Houses

Birthstones. *See* Gems

Blacksmithing

Blind

Blood banks. *See* Hospitals — U. S. — Blood banks

Boats
    See also Iceboats; Steamboats
    Barge
    Basket
    Canal
    Canoe
    Ferry
    Galleon
    Galley
    Primitive
    Raft
    Row
    Speed
    Tug
    Umiak

Bolivia

Bomb shelters. *See* Civilian defense

Bookbinding

Bookmarks

Books
    See also Printing
    Covers
    Fore-edge paintings
    Horn book
    Illumination
    Incunabula
    Plates
    Preface
    Title page

Books and reading. *See* illustrations; name of individual painting, etc.

Borneo

Bornholm

Bosnia. *See* Yugoslavia

Botany

Bottles

Bowling. *See* Games — Bowling

Boxing. *See* Sports — Boxing

Boy scouts

Brazil

Brewing

Brick

Bridge (game). *See* Games — Cards

Bridge-building

Bridges
Covered
Foreign (divided by name of country)
Natural
U. S. (divided by name of state)

British Honduras. *See* Honduras, British

British New Guinea. *See* New Guinea, British

Broadsides. *See* Printing

Brownies

Buddhism

Building materials
See also Brick; Concrete; Stone; etc.

Buildings

Bulgaria

Bull fights. *See* Sports — Bull fights

Burma

Butterflies
  See also Moths

Buoys

Buttons

C

Cables

Cacao. *See* Cocoa

Cactus

Cafés. *See* Restaurants

Calendars

*California (subdivided by county and city)
  Agriculture
  Airports. *See* under names of cities, subdivision Airport
  Animals
  Architecture
  Art galleries and museums
  Arts and crafts
  Beaches
  Birds
  Bridges
  Cemeteries
  Churches. *See also* California — Missions
  Cities and towns
  Clubs
  Colleges and universities
  Court houses
  Customs

Desert
Drama
Fairs
Festivals
Fiestas
Flowers
Gardens
Harbors
History
Hospitals
Industries
Lakes
Libraries
Maps
Minerals
Mines
Missions
Mountains
Moving pictures
Parks and recreation
Portraits (A–Z)
Products
Ranches
Resources
Rivers
Schools. *See also* California — Colleges **and universities**
Sculpture
Social conditions
Sports and games
Theatres
Trades
Transportation
Water supply

Cameos
See also Gems

Camouflage

Camphor

Camping.   *See* Sports — Camping

Canada
  See also Labrador
  Alberta
  British Columbia
  Manitoba
  New Brunswick
  Northwest Territories
  Nova Scotia
  Ontario
  Prince Edward Island
  Quebec
  Saskatchewan
  Yukon

Canal Zone

Canals (subdivided by name of canal)

Canary Islands

Canasta (game)   *See* Games — Cards

Candles

Canning

Canoeing.   *See* Sports — Canoeing

Cape Verde Peninsula

Cards (game)   *See* Games — Cards

Cards.   *See* Greeting cards

Carnivals.   *See* Festivals

Carriages

Cartoons
  Animal
  Animated
  Foreign
  Political
  U. S.
  War

Carving
Ivory
Soap
Stone
Wood

Casinos

Castles (subdivided by adjective of nationality and further by name of castle)

Catacombs. *See* Tombs

Catastrophes. *See* Disasters

Cathedrals (subdivided by adjective of nationality and further by name of cathedral)

Cats (subdivided by types, A–Z)

Cavalry

Cave dwellers and cave dwellings

Caves

Celebes

Celebrations. *See* Expositions; Fairs; Festivals; name of holiday

Cells

Cemeteries
Arlington

Censorship

Central America. *See* Costa Rica; Guatemala; Honduras, British; Nicaragua; Panama; Salvador, El

Ceramics. *See* Pottery

Ceylon

Charcoal drawings. *See* Drawing — Crayon

Chariots

Checkers.   *See* Games — Checkers

Cheese

Chemistry

Chemistry in war

Cherubs
  See also Symbolic pictures — Cherubs; name of painting

Chess.   *See* Games — Chess

Chicago — World's Fair, 1933, 1934.   *See* Expositions — Chicago — World's Fair, 1933, 1934

Children
  See also Babies; name of painting and sculpture

Chile

China

Chinaware.   *See* Pottery

Chivalry.   *See* Armor; Costume — Medieval; Crusades; England — History; France — History; Knights and knighthood; Middle ages; Tournaments; name of individual painting, etc.

Chosen.   *See* Korea

Christmas.   *See also* Bible — Christ; Designs — Christmas; Madonnas; name of individual painting
  Cribs
  Customs
  Decorations

Churches (subdivided by adjective of nationality)
  See also Abbeys; Cathedrals; Missions
  Catholic
  Ismalic
  Jewish
  Protestant (subdivided by denomination)

Ciphers and codes

Circus
See also Costume — Clown

Civilian defense

Civilians in war

Civilization
See also Antiquities; Archaeology; Art; Costume; Egypt, Ancient; Greece, Ancient; Man, Prehistoric; Middle Ages; Rome, Ancient

Clay products
See also Brick
Hollow tile
Terra cotta

Cliff dwellers and dwellings

Clocks
See also Watches

Closets

Clothing. *See* Costume

Clouds

Coal mines and mining

Coal-tar products

Coasting. *See* Sports — Coasting

Coats of arms (subdivided by name of country, etc.)
See also Seals; Symbolic pictures

Cocoa

Coffee

Coffee houses

Coins (subdivided by adjective of nationality)

Colleges and universities (subdivided by name of state)

Colombia

Colonial life and customs
See also Costume — American — 1607–1783 (Colonial);
Pilgrim fathers; U. S. — History — Colonial period
Agriculture
Architecture
Arts and crafts
Churches
Cities
Clothing. *See* Costume — American — 1607–1783 (Colonial)
Community life
Cookery
Dancing
Education
Food
Furniture
Government
Heating methods
Indian relations
Industries
Lighting methods
Maps
Middle colonies
Money substitutes
Needlework
New England
New York
Pennsylvania
Pilgrims. *See* Pilgrim Fathers
Postal service
Recreation
Religious customs
Resources
Roads and streets
Schools
Shelter

Slavery
Social conditions
South
Spinning and weaving
Taverns
Thanksgiving
Tools
Trade
Transportation
Villages and towns
Weapons
Workers

Color

Colombia

Colorado

Communication. *See* various types of communication

Compass

Concrete

Congo, Belgian

Connecticut

Conscription

Constitution of U. S. *See* U. S. — Constitution

Contraband

Conventions

Convents

Convoy

Cookery

Copper

Coral

Cork

Corn

Corsica

Cosmetics

Costa Rica

*Costume (subdivided under country by century)
 See also Fans; Hats; etc. names of paintings
 Abyssinian
 Afghan
 African
 Albanian
 Algerian
 American
   1607–1783 (Colonial)
   1783–1825
   Subdivided by year after 1825
 Ancient
 Arabian
 Armor
 Assyrian
 Austrian
 Baby
 Baker
 Bakst
 Balkan
 Barbaric
 Barber
 Bavarian
 Bathing
 Belgian
 Biblical. *See also* Bible
 Bolivian
 Bulgarian
 Burmese
 Byzantine
 Cavalier

Central American
Child
Chinese
Clown
College
Cook
Cowboy
Cuban
Czechoslovakian
Danish
Design
Devil
Dutch
Ecclesiastical
Egyptian
Elizabethan
English
Eskimo
Fancy dress
Fireman
Fisherman
Flemish
French
Frontier
Furs
German
Gipsy
Gloves
Greek
  Ancient
  Modern
Hawaiian
Head dress
Hungarian
Indian
  East
  Incan
  North American (subdivided by name of tribe)
  South American (subdivided by name of tribe)

Irish
Italian
Japanese
Javanese
Jester
Jewish
Jugo-Slav. *See* Yugoslav
Knit
Korean
Lithuanian
Madeiran
Maid
Malaysian
Maori
Medieval (476 A.D. — 1492)
Mexican
Military
  Arabian
  British
  English
  French
  German
  Greek
  Italian
  Japanese
  Scotch
  Spanish
  Swiss
Miller
Minstrel
Mongolian
Moroccan
Norwegian
Nurse
Operas (subdivided by name of opera)
Organ grinder
Page
Palestinian
Patriotic

Persian
Philippine
Phoenician
Pioneer
Pirate
Polar region
Polish
Porter
Portuguese
Prince (subdivided by adjective of nationality)
Puritan
    See also Costume — American — 1607–1783 (Colonial)
Quaker
Queen
Rainwear
Renaissance
Riding
Roman
Royal
Rumanian
Russian
Sailor
Scotch
Scout, Boy
Scout, Girl
Servant
Shepherd
Shoemaker
Shoes
Siamese
Siberian
Sicilian
South American
Spanish
Sport
Stage (subdivided by author and title of play)
Swedish
Swiss

Syrian
Tibetan
Tudor
Tunisian
Turkish
Uniforms
Victorian
Wedding
Welsh
Yugoslav

Cotton

Country life

Covered wagons.   *See* Transportation — History

Cowboys

Cricket.   *See* Games — Cricket

Croquet.   *See* Games — Croquet

Crosses

Crowns

Cruisers

Crusades

Cuba

Curling.   *See* Games — Curling

Currency
   See also Coins

Cutlery

Cyclones

Cyclotrons

Czechoslovakia

D

Dairying

Dams (subdivided by name of dam)

Dances (subdivided by name of dance)
Ballet

Deaf

Decoration. *See* Design; Lettering; Painting; **Pottery;** etc.

Decoration Day. *See* Memorial Day

Defense. *See* Civilian defense; War defense

Delaware

Denmark
See also Bornholm; Funen; Jutland; Zealand

Dentistry
See also Teeth

Desert
See also Arabia; Egypt — Sahara; etc.
Agriculture
Arts and crafts
Community and family life
Herdsmen
Oases
Shelters
Trade
Transportation
Water

Design
African
All-over
Animal (subdivided by name of animal)
Arabian

Assyrian
Astronomy
Aztec
Baroque
Bird (subdivided by name of bird)
Block printing
Border
Branch
Byzantine
Card and label
Cartouche
Celtic
Chinese
Christmas
Circle
Classical
Colonial
Container
Copper
Corner
Czechoslovak
Dragon
Easter
Egyptian
English
Etruscan
Figure
Fish
Flat. *See* Design — Surface
Flower (subdivided by name of flower)
French
Frieze
Fruit (subdivided by name of fruit)
Geometric
German
Glass
Gothic
Greek
Hawaiian

Horn of plenty
Hungarian
Indian, American
Indian, East
Indian, Mexican
Industrial
Insect
Italian
Japanese
Labyrinth
Leaf
Leather
Lettering
Medallion
Medieval
Menu card
Modern
Musical
Oriental.   *See also* Chinese; Japanese; etc.
Panel
Peasant
Persian
Peruvian
Plastic
Pompeian
Prehistoric
Renaissance
Rococo
Roman
Romanesque
Rosette
Russian
Ruthenian
Saracenic
Scandinavian
Scroll
Sea life
Sicilian
Spanish

Square
Stencil
Surface
Symbolic
Textile
Tree
Turkish
Vignette
Visiting card
Wall and ceiling
Wall paper. *See* Wall papers

Dials

Diamonds

Disasters
See also Aircraft accidents; Accidents; Cyclones; Earthquakes; Explosions; Fires; Floods; Hurricanes; Railroads — Accidents; Shipwrecks; Storms; Tidal waves; Tornadoes; Typhoons; Volcanoes

Discoveries (in geography). *See* America — Discovery and exploration; Arctic regions; etc.

District of Columbia

Dogs (subdivided by type, A–Z)

Dogs in war

Dolls

Dominican Republic

Draperies

Drawing
Animal
Blackboard
Brush
Crayon
Figure

Foot
Hand
Head
Pen and ink
Perspective
Stipple

*Drawings and engravings (subdivided by name of artist, and further by name of drawing)

Driving. *See* Sports — Driving

Drugs

Dutch East Indies. *See* Netherlands Indies

Dwarfs

E

Earthquakes

Easter

Ecuador

Education. *See* Schools

Egypt
See also Art — Egyptian; Costume — Egyptian; Pyramids; etc.
Antiquities
Civilization
Monuments
Mummies
Sahara

Eire

El Salvador. *See* Salvador, El

Elections

Electric power plants

Electricity

Emblems

Enamels

Engineering

England
History

Engraving process
See also Etching process
Banknote
Copper
Linoleum
Steel
Wood

Engravings.   *See* Drawings and engravings

Erasers
See also Pencils, Lead

Eritrea

Eskimos

Estonia

Etching process

Etchings.   *See* Drawings and engravings

Ethiopia

Europe.   *See* name of individual country: Albania; etc.

European war, 1914–1918
See also under name of individual country

European war, 1939–1945
See also under name of individual country

Exhibitions.   *See* Museums

Explorations
See also America — Discovery and exploration; Arctic regions

Exploring. *See* Sports — Exploring

Explosions

Expositions
Alaska — Yukon, 1909
Brussels, 1910
California Pacific International Exposition, San Diego, 1935
Centennial, 1876
Chicago — World's Fair, 1933, 1934
Columbian, 1893
Festival of Britain, 1951
Jamestown, 1907
Lewis and Clark, 1905
Louisiana Purchase, 1904
Milan, 1906
New York City World's Fair, 1939–1940
Pageant of the Pacific, San Francisco, 1939–1940
Pan American, 1901
Panama Pacific, 1915
Paris, 1897
Paris, 1900
Paris, 1925
Philadelphia, 1926
Quebec, 1908
Texas Centennial, 1936
Tokio, 1922
Turin, 1911
Wimbledon, 1924

F

Factories

Fairs

Fans

Farm life. *See* Country life

Fats and oils

Feathers

Fencing. *See* Sports — Fencing

Ferns

Festivals
  See also name of festival

Fibers
  See also Cotton; Flax; Hemp; Linen; Nylon; Silk; Textiles; Wool; etc.

Fiji Islands

Finger prints

Finland

Firearms. *See* Guns

Fireplaces
  See also Barbecues
  Accessories
  Mantels
  Modern

Fires

Fireworks

First aid

Fisheries

Fishes (subdivided by name of fish)
  Aquariums

Fishing (Industry)
  See also Pearl fishing; Whaling

Fishing (Sport). *See* Sports — Fishing

Flag Day

Flags

Flax

Floats

Floods

Florida

Flour and flour mills

Flower arrangement

Flowers (subdivided by name of flower)

Fog

Food
  See also Berries; Fruit; Meat; Nuts; Vegetables; etc.

Football. *See* Games — Football

Forestry
  See also Fires
  Conservation

Forging. *See* Blacksmithing

Formosa

Forts

Fossils

Fountains
  See also Sculpture

Fourth of July

France
  See also Madagascar
  History

French Pacific Settlements

Frontier and pioneer life

Fruit (subdivided by name of fruit)
  See also Berries

Fruit growing

Funen (Island)

Funerals (subdivided by adjective of nationality)
  Military
  Naval

Fungi

Furniture (subdivided further by name of piece)
  African
  American
    Colonial
    Duncan Phyfe
    Empire
  Ancient
  Built-in
  Chinese
  Chinese Chippendale
  Czechoslovak
  Danish
  Dutch
  Ecclesiastical
  Egyptian
  English
    Charles II
    Elizabethan
    Georgian
      Adam
      Chippendale
      Heppelwhite
      Sheraton
    Gothic. *See* Furniture — Gothic
    Jacobean
    Norman. *See* Furniture — Norman

Queen Anne
Renaissance
Saxon
William and Mary
Finnish
French
  Louis XIV
  Louis XV
  Louis XVI
  Empire
French provincial
Garden
German
Gothic
Inlaid
Italian
  Renaissance
Japanese
Lacquered
Marquetry
Metal
Mission
Modern
Monterey
Norman
Norwegian
Painted
Porch
Reed
Regency
Russian
Scandinavian
Spanish
Victorian
Welsh
Wicker
Willow

Furs

G

Gadgets

*Games
Baseball
Basketball
Battledore and shuttlecock
Billiards
Bowling
Cards
Checkers
Chess
Cricket
Croquet
Curling
Football
Golf
Hockey
Lacrosse
Leap frog
Marbles
Musical chairs
Olympic
Polo
Roulette
Stilts
Tennis

Gardens
American
Arbor
Chinese
City
Color
Cypress
Desert
English
Fence
Formal

French
Furniture.   *See* Furniture — Garden
Gate
German
Greenhouses
Hedge and topiary
Hillside
Historic
Houses
Indoor.   *See* Gardens — Miniature
Informal
Italian
Japanese
Landscape
Miniature
Ornament
Path
Pergola
Persian
Plans
Pond
Pool
Rock
Roof
Rose
Scandinavian
Seaside
Seats
Spanish
Steps
Sunken
Terrace
U. S.
Vegetable
Victory
Walk
Wall
Water
Window

Gates
See also Gardens — Gate

Gems
See also name of individual gem

Geology

Georgia

Germany

Gesso

Geysers

Ghost towns

Ghosts

Giants

Gibraltar

Gipsies

Girl scouts

Glaciers

Glass, Stained

Glassware (subdivided by adjective of nationality)
See also Bottles
Modern
Pressed
Sandwich
Stiegel
Venetian

Gliders

Gobi desert

Gold mines and mining

Goldsmithing

Golf. *See* Games — Golf

Gourds

Graduations

Grains and grasses
See also Corn; Wheat; etc.

Granite. *See* Quarrying

Graves. *See* Cemeteries; Funerals; Tombs

Great Britain. *See* England; Ireland; Scotland; Wales; etc.

Great Lakes

Greece

Greece, Ancient
Agriculture
Alphabet
Antiquities
Architecture. *See* Architecture — Greek
Art. *See* Art — Greek
Athens
Chariot races
Clothing
Communication
Costume. *See* Costume — Greek — Ancient
Drama and festivals
Education
Food
Gateways
Government
Gymnasiums
Heating methods
Home life
Houses
Industries
Language
Lighting

Maps
Market place
Money
Music
Olympic games
Parthenon
Recreation
Religion
Shelter
Slaves
Social life
Theatres
Transportation
Walls
Workers
Writing

Greenhouses

Greenland

Greeting cards (subdivided by name of holiday)
Comic
Foreign
Photographic
Religious

Grotesques

Guadalcanal

Guam

Guatemala

Guerrilla warfare

Guiana, British

Guiana, French

Guinea, Portugese

Guinea, Spanish

Guns

Gymnastics
See also Games; Sports; etc.

Gypsies. *See* Gipsies

Gyroscopes

H

Haiti

Hallowe'en

Handicrafts. *See* Arts and Crafts; name of individual
handicraft

Hangars
Airplane
Dirigible

Hardware

Harvest. *See* Agriculture; Autumn; Corn; Thanksgiving;
Wheat; etc.

Hats

Hawaiian Islands

Heating
See also Fireplaces
Prehistoric methods
Stoves

Helicopters

Hemp

Heraldry. *See* Books — Plates; Coats of arms

Hieroglyphics

Highways

Historic gardens. *See* Gardens — Historic

*Historic houses

*Historic landmarks

*Historic relics

Hobbies
See also Arts and crafts; name of individual hobby

Hockey. *See* Games — Hockcy

Holidays. *See* name of holiday

Holland. *See* Netherlands

Honduras

Honduras, British

Honey. *See* Bee-keeping

Horn Book. *See* Books — Horn Book

Horoscopes. *See* Astrology

Horses (subdivided by types, A–Z)
Racing
Riding
Shows

Hospitals
Foreign
U. S. (subdivided by name of city)
Blood banks
Children's
Maternity
Mental
Operations
Veteran's

Hotels (subdivided by adjective of nationality)

Hour glasses

House boats

Household appliances (subdivided by name of appliance)
See also Gadgets

Houses — Exterior. *See* Architecture

Houses — Interior. *See* Interior decoration

Housing
See also Slums
Foreign
U. S. (subdivided by name of city)

Hungary

Hunting. *See* Sports — Hunting

Hurricanes

Hypnotism

I

Ice

Icebergs

Ice-boating. *See* Sports — Ice-boating

Iceboats

Iceland

Idaho

Idols

Illinois

*Illustrations
Bible

Inaugurations

India
   See also Pakistan

Indiana

Indians (subdivided by name of tribe)
   Agriculture
   Arts and crafts
   Basketry
   Ceremonies
   Children
   Clothing.   *See* Costume — Indian
   Communication
   Cookery
   Dances
   Education
   Family and community life
   Fishing
   Food
   Games and Sports
   Hunting
   Missions
   Pottery
   Reservations
   Shelter
   Transportation
   Utensils
   Village
   Warfare
   Weapons and tools
   Weaving
   Writing

Indigo

Indo-Chinese Federation
   See also Burma; Siam; etc.

Indonesia
   See also Celebes; Sumatra

Industries.   *See* name of industry

Infantry. *See* Army — U. S. — Infantry

Inns (subdivided by adjective of nationality)
 U. S. (subdivided by name of inn)

Insects (subdivided by name of insect)

Insignia (subdivided by adjective of nationality)
 U. S. (subdivided by state)
  Army (subdivided by division)
  Civilian defense
  Navy

Intelligence

Interior decoration (subdivided by name of period)
 See also Furniture

Inventions

Iowa

Iran

Iraq

Ireland
 See also Eire; Northern Ireland

Iron

Irrigation

Islands. *See* name of island

Isle of Man

Israel

Italian Somaliland

Italy

Ivory
 See also Carving — Ivory

J

Jade

Jamaica

Japan
  See also Formosa; **etc.**

Japanese

Japanese prints. *See* Art — Japanese

Java

Jet propulsion

Jewelry
  African
  Ancient
  Anglo-Saxon
  Arabian
  Byzantine
  Celtic
  Chinese
  Dutch
  Egyptian
  Frankish
  French
  German
  Gothic
  Greek
  Hungarian
  Indian
  Italian
  Japanese
  Manufacture
  Medieval
  Modern (subdivided by name of piece)
  Persian
  Portuguese
  Renaissance

Roman
Russian
Scandinavian
Trojan

Jewels. *See* Gems

Jews

Jordan

Journalism

Jugoslavia. *See* Yugoslavia

Jungle
   See also name of tropical country

Jutland

K

Kansas

Kentucky
   Mammoth Cave

Kenya

Kites

Knights and knighthood

Knots and splices

Kongo, Belgian. *See* Congo, Belgian

Korea (Chosen)

Ku Klux Klan

L

Laboratories
Labrador

Lace

Lacrosse. *See* Games — Lacrosse

Lake dwellers and lake dwellings
  See also House boats

Lakes
  See also Great Lakes ; name of country, etc.

Lamps
  See also Lanterns
Landscape gardening. *See* Gardens

Landscapes. *See* name of individual painting

Lanterns

Lapland

Latvia

Lead

Leap frog. *See* Games — Leap frog

Leather
  See also Design — Leather

Lebanon

Lettering
  Block
  Chinese
  Composition
  English, Old
  Engraved
  Fancy
  Gothic
  Initial
  Italic and script
  Japanese
  Manuscript
  Modern

Monograms
Renaissance
Roman
Showcard

Liberia

Libraries (subdivided by adjective of nationality; U. S. also subdivided by name of state)

Libya

Liechtenstein

Life saving
Stations

Lighthouses

Lighting
See also Lamps; Lanterns

Lightning

Linen
Household

Linoleum

Lithographs.   *See* Drawings and engravings

Lithuania

Looms.   *See* Spinning; Weaving

Louisiana

Lumbering

Luxemburg

Luzon

M

Machinery (subdivided by name of machine)
See also Agricultural machinery; Tools; Weapons

Madagascar

Madeira

Madonnas
   See also name of individual painting, sculpture, etc.

Maine

Malta

Mammoth Cave.   *See* Kentucky — Mammoth Cave

Man, Isle of.   *See* Isle of Man

Man, Prehistoric
   See also Art — Prehistoric; Cliff dwellers and dwellings;
   Lake dwellers and lake dwellings; Stone age; Tools —
   Prehistoric; etc.

Manchuria

Manuscripts
   See also Books — Illumination; Writing — History of

Maple sugar.   *See* Sugar — Maple

Maps.   *See* World — Maps; under name of country, subdivision Maps

Maps, Decorative

Marbles.   *See* Games — Marbles

Mardi Gras

Marines — U. S.

Marionettes
   See also Puppet plays

Maryland

Masks

Massachusetts

May Day

Meat

Meat industry and trade

Medals
See also name of individual sculpture

Memorial Day

Memorials (subdivided by name of person)
See also Fountains; Monuments; Taj Mahal; Tombs; name of individual sculpture; etc.

Mesopotamia. *See* Iraq

Metalwork
American
Arabic
Architectural
Austrian
Brass and copper
Bronze
Chinese
Danish
Design
Dutch
Ecclesiastical
English
Engraved
Flemish
French
German
Indian, American
Indian, East
Italian
Japanese
Roman
Russian
South American
Spanish
Tibetan

Mexico

Michigan

Microscopy

Middle Ages
    See also Chivalry; Crusades; Knights and knighthood;
    Tournaments
    Agriculture
    Animals
    Architecture. *See* Architecture — Medieval
    Armor
    Art. *See* Art — Medieval
    Banks
    Books
    Castles
    Cathedrals
    Ceremonies
    Churches
    Cities and towns
    Clothing
    Communication
    Crime and criminals
    Dentistry
    Eating customs
    Education
    Exploration and discovery
    Fairs and expositions
    Falconry
    Feudalism
    Fire brigade
    Food
    Freedom
    Furniture
    Gilds
    Government
    Heating methods
    Hospitals
    Hunting

Industries
Maps
Markets
Monasteries
Money
Monks
Musical instruments
Newspapers
Pilgrims and pilgrimages
Progress
Recreation
Religion
Sanitation
Science
Sculpture
Shelter
Social conditions
Taverns and inns
Teutonic tribes
Trade
Transportation
Travel
Warfare
Water supply
Weapons
Writing

Midway Islands

Mills
See also Windmills; name of individual painting

Mines and mineral resources
See also Coal mines and mining; Gold mines and mining; etc.

Minnesota

Minorities

Mirrors

Missions

Mississippi

Missouri

Monaco

Monasteries

Money. *See* Coins; Currency

Mongolia

Monks

Montana

Montenegro. *See* Yugoslavia

Monuments (subdivided by names of person)
See also Memorials; Tombs; names of individual sculpture

Moon. *See* Astronomy

Morocco

Mosaics (subdivided by name of artist)

Mosques. *See* Churches — Ismalic

Moths. *See also* Butterflies

Mound builders and mounds

Mountain climbing. *See* Sports — Mountain climbing

Mountains. *See* name of individual country

Moving pictures

Mummies

Mural paintings. *See* name of individual painting

Museums (subdivided by adjective of nationality)

Music

Musical chairs. *See* Games — Musical chairs

Musical instruments (subdivided by name of instrument)

Mythology (subdivided by name of god and goddess)
Celtic
Egyptian
German
Greek and Roman
Indian, American
Indian, East
Japanese
Norse
Persian

N

National conventions (political)

Navigation. *See* Boats; Cruisers; Ships; Ships, Historic; Steamboats; U. S. — Navy; Warships; etc.

Navy (subdivided as in Army — U. S.)
U. S.

Near East

Nebraska

Needlework
Appliqué
Bag
Chair
Crochet
Cross-stitch
Cutwork
Embroidery (subdivided by adjective of nationality)
Knitting
Monograms
Needlepoint
Pillow-cover
Quilt and bedspread
Sampler
Table cover

Negroes

Nepal

Netherlands

Netherlands Indies

Nevada

New Caledonia

New Guinea

New Guinea, British

New Guinea, Dutch

New Hampshire

New Hebrides

New Jersey

New Mexico

New Year

New York

New Zealand
  North Island
  South Island

Newfoundland
  See also Labrador

Newspaper work.   *See* Journalism

Newspapers

Nicaragua

Nigeria

Night clubs

North Carolina

North Dakota

North Island. *See* New Zealand — North Island

Northern Ireland

Norway

Nova Scotia

Nuts (subdivided by name of nut)

Nylon

O

Observatories. *See* Astronomical observatories

Occupations

Ocean

Oceania

Ohio

Oil wells. *See* Petroleum

Oklahoma

Olympic games. *See* Games — Olympic

Operas

Orchestras

Oregon

Outer Mongolia

P

Pacific Islands. *See* Oceania

Pageants

*Paintings (subdivided by name of painter and further by name of painting)

Pakistan

Palaces (subdivided by adjective of nationality and further by name of palace)

Palestine

Panama

Paper making and trade

Parachutes

Parades

Paraguay

Parks
See also Gardens

Passion Play

Patriotic pictures
See also name of individual painting and sculpture

Pearl fishing

Pencils, Lead
See also Erasers

Pennsylvania

Persia. *See* Iran

Peru

Petroleum

Pewter (subdivided by adjective of nationality)

Philippines, Republic of

Phosphates

Photography

Pigmies
See also New Guinea, Dutch

Pilgrim Fathers

Pipes

Planetariums (subdivided by adjectives of nationality)

Plantation life
  See also Cotton; Negroes; South; name of southern state

Plants (subdivided by name of plant)

Plastics

Poland

Polo. *See* Games — Polo

Porcelain. *See* Pottery

Portraits (subdivided by name of person)

Portugal

Post offices

Postage stamps

Postal service — History

Pottery (subdivided by adjective of nationality and further
    by name of pottery)

Poultry. *See* Birds

Poultry houses

Power (Mechanics)
  See also Atomic energy; Electric power plants; Water
  power

Prehistoric animals. *See* Animals, Prehistoric

Prehistoric man

Prehistoric sculpture. *See* Sculpture, Prehistoric

Printing
  Broadsides
  Colophons
  Color
  Display
  Head and tail pieces
  History
  Initials
  Letterheads
  Pamphlet covers
  Presses
  Process
  Publishing houses
  Title page
  Type face
  Type page

Prisoners of war

Prisons

Propaganda

Puerto Rico

Punishments

Puppet plays

Puritans. *See* Costume — American — 1607–1783; Pilgrim fathers

Pyramids

Q

Quakers

Quarrying

R

Races of man
  Black
  Brown

Prehistoric. *See* Man, Prehistoric
Red
White
Yellow

Racing. *See* Sports — Racing

Radar

Radio in war

Radios

Railroads
  Accidents
  Elevated
  Signals
  Stations
  Subway
  Trains
  Wrecks

Rain

Rationing

Recreation. *See* Games; Sports

Red Cross

Religious pictures. *See* Bible; Bible-Christ; Illustrations — Bible; Madonnas; Passion Play; Symbolic pictures

Reproduction

Reptiles. *See* Animals

Rescues

Restaurants

Rhode Island

Riding. *See* Sports — Riding

Riots

Rites and ceremonies

Rivers. *See* under name of country, subdivision name of
    rivers

Roads (subdivided by name of country)

Rocks

Roller-skating.   *See* Sports — Roller-skating

Rome, Ancient
   Agriculture
   Antiquities
   Appian Way
   Aqueduct
   Arches
   Army and Navy
   Baths
   Burial customs
   Business
   Circus Maximus
   Clothing
   Costume
   Communication
   Education
   Empire
   Engineering
   Food
   Forum
   Harbor
   Heating methods
   Home life
   Houses
   Industries
   Maps
   Military and naval operations
   Pantheon
   Postal service and post roads
   Recreation

Religion
Roads
Shelter
Social conditions
Soldiers
Tabularium
Temples
Tools and weapons
Transportation
Treasury
Workers

Rope

Roulette. *See* Games — Roulette

Rowing. *See* Sports — Rowing

Rubber

Rugs (subdivided by adjective of nationality and further by type of rug)

Rumania

Russia. *See* Union of Soviet Socialist Republics

S

Sabotage

Sahara. *See* Egypt — Sahara

Sailing. *See* Sports — Sailing

Saints

Salt

Salvador, El

Samoa, American. *See* American Samoa

San Marino

Sand

Sardinia

Saudi Arabia, Kingdom of

Scales. *See* Weights and measures

Scandinavia. *See* Denmark; Norway; Sweden

Schools (subdivided by adjective of nationality)

Science
  See also name of individual Science, e.g. Astronomy

Scouts and scouting. *See* Boy scouts; Girl scouts

Scotland

Screens

*Sculpture (subdivided by name of artist, and further by name of individual sculpture)
  Prehistoric

Sea life
  See also Fishes

Seadromes. *See* Airports, Floating

Seals
  City
  College
  State. *See also* Coats of arms

Seaplanes

Seascapes
  See also name of individual painting

Seasons
  See also name of season, e.g. Autumn

Seeds
  See also Flowers; Plants; Trees

Seven Wonders of the World
  See also Pyramids

Sewers

Shawls
  Indian
  Kashmir
  Paisley

Shells

Shelter. *See* name of country, e.g. Greece, Ancient

Shipbuilding

Ships (subdivided by adjective of nationality)
  See also Boats; Cruisers; Steamboats; Warships; name
  of individual painting, etc.
  Historic
  Models

Shipwrecks

Shrines

Shrubs (subdivided by name of shrub)

Siam

Siberia

Sicily

Signaling
  Arm
  Aviation
  Buoy
  Drum
  Fire
  Flag
  Heliograph
  Indian
  Lighthouse

Lightship
Megaphone
Radio
Semaphore
Ship
Sight
Smoke
Sound
Swiss
Telegraph call
Telephone switchboard
Thermometer bells
Traffic lights
Visibility
Wigwag

Silhouettes

Silk

Silverware (subdivided by adjective of nationality)

Skating.   *See* Sports — Skating

Skeletons
Skulls

Skiing.   *See* Sports — Skiing

Skyscrapers

Slavery
See also Negroes; Plantation life; South; U. S. — History — Civil War

Slums

Smog

Snow

Snow crystals

Soap

Social settlements

South

South America. *See* Argentina; Bolivia; Brazil; Chile; Colombia; Ecuador; Panama; Paraguay; Peru; Uruguay; Venezuela

South Carolina

South Dakota

South Island. *See* New Zealand — South Island

Spain

Spices (subdivided by name of spice)

Spinning

Spitzbergen

Sponges

*Sports
  See also Games
  Acrobatics
  Archery
  Bicycling
  Boxing
  Bull fights
  Camping
  Canoeing
  Coasting
  Driving
  Exploring
  Fencing
  Fishing
  Greek and Roman
  Hunting
  Ice-boating
  Mountain climbing
  Racing
  Riding

Roller-skating
Rowing
Sailing
Skating
Skiing
Swimming
Winter
Wrestling

Spring
See also Symbolic pictures — Seasons — Spring; names of individual paintings

Stage
See also Costume — Stage; Illustrations; Theatre; etc.
Settings

Stage coaches. *See* Transportation — History

Stained glass. *See* Glass, Stained

Stamps. *See* Postage stamps

Stations. *See* Railroads — Stations

Statues. *See* Memorials; Monuments; Sculpture

Steamboats

Steel

Still life. *See* name of individual painting

Stilts. *See* Games — Stilts

Stock raising

Stock yards

Stone

Stone Age
See also Man, Prehistoric
New Stone Age
Old Stone Age

Stone carving. *See* Carving — Stone

Storms
   See also Cyclones; Hurricanes; Tornadoes; etc.

Straits Settlements

Strikes

Structures, Famous
   See also Bridges; Buildings; Monuments; Pyramids;
   Seven Wonders of the World; etc.
   Ancient
   Asiatic
   European
   United States

Submarine warfare

Submarines

Sugar
   Beet
   Cane
   Maple

Sumatra

Summer
   See also Symbolic pictures — Seasons — Summer; name
   of individual painting

Sundials. *See* Dials

Sunrise
   See also name of individual painting

Sunset
   See also name of individual painting

Surgery

Sweden

Swimming. *See* Sports — Swimming

Swimming pools

Switzerland

Swords

Symbolic pictures
Abundance
Agriculture
Angels
Architecture
Art
Aspiration
Astronomy
Avarice
Beauty
Carnival
Charity
Cherubs
Church
Cities
Civic virtue
Civilization
Coats of arms
Commerce
Communication
Continents
Countries (subdivided by name of country)
Courage
Dance
Death
Disease
Drama
Drink
Earth
Electricity
Elements
Emotions (subdivided by name of emotion)
Faith
Faithfulness

Fame
Fanaticism
Fate
Fauns
Friendship
Gardening
Geography
Geology
Glory
Habit
Happiness
Harmony
Harvest
Health
Heaven
Hell
Heroism
History
Hope
Hunger
Immortality
Indolence
Industries
Industry
Innocence
Inspiration
Jealousy
Justice
Knowledge
Lakes
Law
Liberty-Tyranny
Life
   Childhood
   Youth
   Maturity
   Old Age
Light
Love

Magnetism
Medicine
Melancholy
Memory
Mercy
Miserliness
Motherhood
Muses
Mythology
Nature
Navigation
Night
Nymphs
Ocean
Painting
Parting
Peace
Philosophy
Piety
Play
Pleasure and cheerfulness
Poetry
Poverty
Progress
Purity
Reconciliation
Religion
Rest
Satan
Satire
Science
Seasons
    Spring
    Summer
    Autumn
    Winter
Senses
Sensuality
Silence

Slavery
Sleep
Song
Sorrow
Sports
Steam
Struggle
Stupidity
Temptation
Thought
Time
Trades
Truth — Lie
Utility
Vanity
Vices
Victory
Virtue
Vision
War
Winds
Wine
Wisdom

Synagogues. *See* Churches — Jewish

Syria

T

Table ware. *See* Beetleware; Glassware; Pewter; Plastics; Pottery; Silverware; etc.

Tablets. *See* Memorials; Monuments; Tombs; name of individual sculpture

Taj Mahal

Tanks
  Military

Tapestries

Tasmania

Taxidermy

Tea

Teeth

Telegraph

Telephone

Telescope

Television

Temples
Assyrian
Babylonian
Chinese
Greek
Indian, **East**
Japanese
Mexican
Mormon
Roman
Syrian

Tennessee

Tennis.   *See* Games — Tennis

Territory of the Pacific Islands

Texas

Textiles
See also Cotton; Design — Textile; Linen; Nylon; Silk;
  Wool
Batik
Brocade
Chintz
Colonial
Cretonne

Primitive
Rayon
Scotch plaids
Trimmings
Veils
Velvets

Thanksgiving
See also Pilgrim Fathers

Theatres (subdivided by adjective of nationality)
See also Costume — Stage; Stage settings

Thousand Islands

Tibet

Tidal waves

Tiles

Time
See also Clocks; Watches

Tobacco

Tombs (subdivided by name of person)
See also Memorials; Monuments; names of individual sculpture

Tools (subdivided by name of tool)
See also Agricultural machinery; Weapons
Prehistoric

Tornadoes

Totem poles

Tournaments

Toys
See also Dolls

Trade marks

Trailers

Trains.   *See* Railroads — Trains

Trans-Jordan

Transportation — History
See also Airplanes; Airports; Airships; Autogiros;
Automobiles; Balloons; Boats; Canals; Carriages;
Cruisers; Railroads; Seaplanes; Ships; ships, Historic;
Steam boats; Submarines; Tanks; Vehicles; Warships;
Water transportation; Yachts and yachting

Tree dwellers and tree dwellings

Trees (subdivided by name of tree)
Blossoms
Historic
Leaves

Trials

Trieste, Free Territory of

Tripoli (Tripolitania)

Tunis

Tunnels (subdivided by name of tunnel)

Turkey

Typewriters

Typhoons

U

Union of South Africa

Union of Soviet Socialist Republics

United Nations

United States
See also Army — U .S.; Marines — U. S.; Navy — U. S.,
name of state

Constitution
Government
  Congress
  Elections
  Inaugurations
  Supreme court
History
  Colonial period
  Revolution
  War of 1812
  Civil War
  Spanish American War
  European War

Universities and colleges (subdivided by country, and in case of U. S., further by name of state)

Uranium

Uruguay

Utah

V

Vatican City

Vaudeville

Vegetables (subdivided by name of vegetable)

Vehicles

Venezuela

Vermont

Veterans

Virgin Islands

Virginia

Volcanoes (subdivided by name of volcano)

W

Wagons.   *See* Transportation — History; Vehicles

Wales

Wall coverings
See also Wall papers

Wall papers

War
See also U. S. — History; name of war

War and art

War defense

Warfare

Warships

Washington

Watches

Water power

Water transportation

Waterfalls

Weapons

Weather
See also Rain; Snow

Weathervanes

Weaving

Weddings

Weeds (subdivided by name of weed)

Weights and measures

Welding
See also Blacksmithing

Wells

West Indies

West Virginia

Western life
See also Frontier and pioneer life; name of western state

Whaling

Wheat

Wight, Isle of

Windmills

Winter
See also Symbolic pictures — Seasons — Winter; name of individual painting

Winter sports. *See* Sports — Winter

Wisconsin

Witches
See also Hallowe'en

Women

Women in war service

Wood

Wood engraving. *See* Engraving process

Woodblock printing. *See* Design — Block printing

Woodcraft

Wool

World — Maps

World Wars. *See* European War, 1914–1918; European War, 1939–1945

Wrestling. *See* Sports — Wrestling

Writing, History of
  See also Hieroglyphics; Lettering; Manuscripts

Wyoming

X

X-Ray

Y

Yachts and yachting

Y. M. C. A.

Y. W. C. A.

Youth

Youth in war

Yugoslavia

Z

Zealand

Zodiac

Zoological gardens

Zoos

INDEX

133

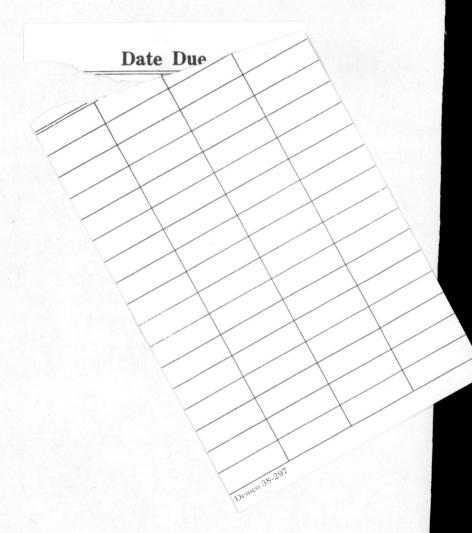

Date Due

Demco 38-297